Animals Coloring Book

PSYCHEDELIC STRESS-RELIEVING ANIMALS

A Coloring Book For Adults

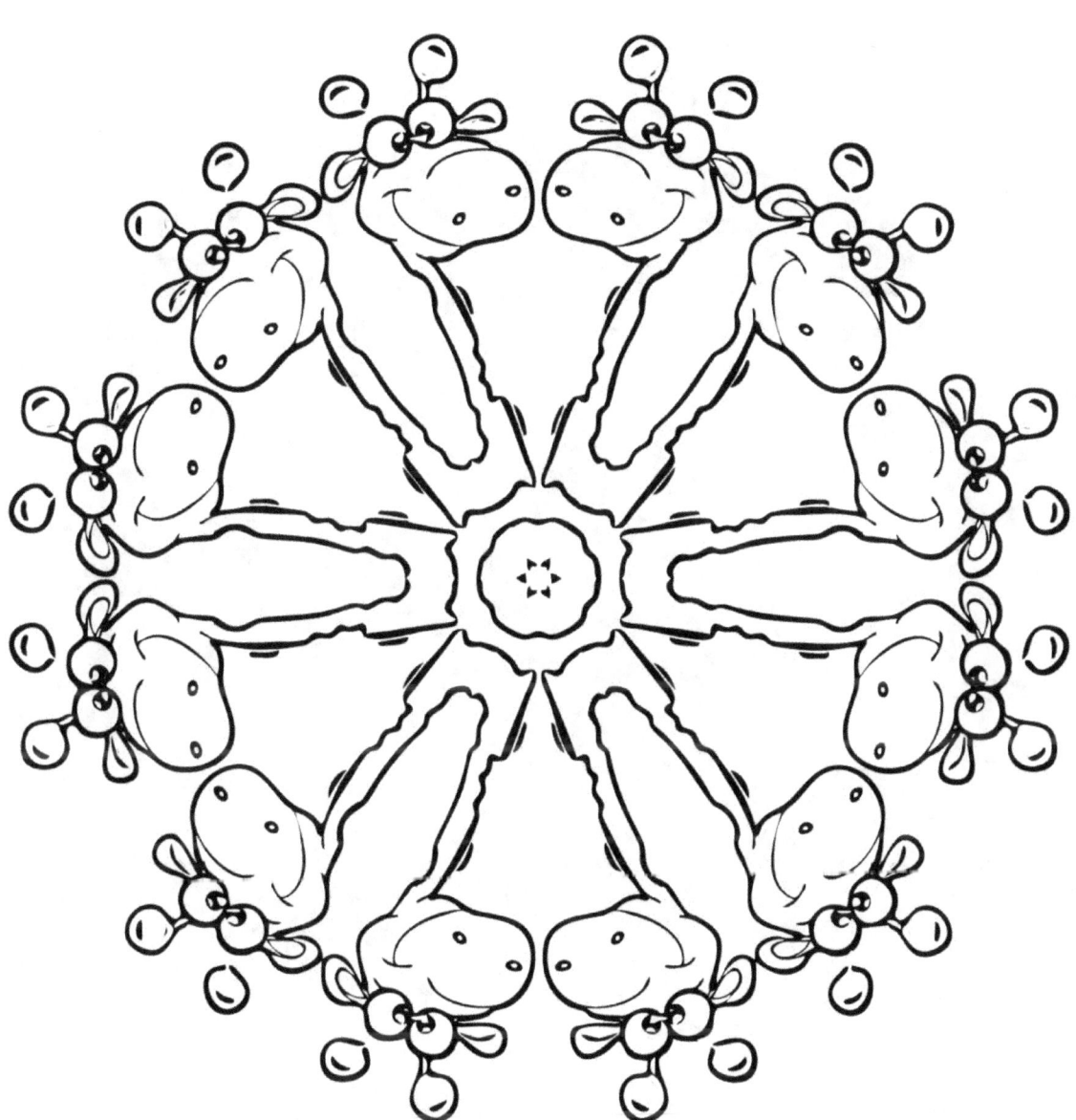

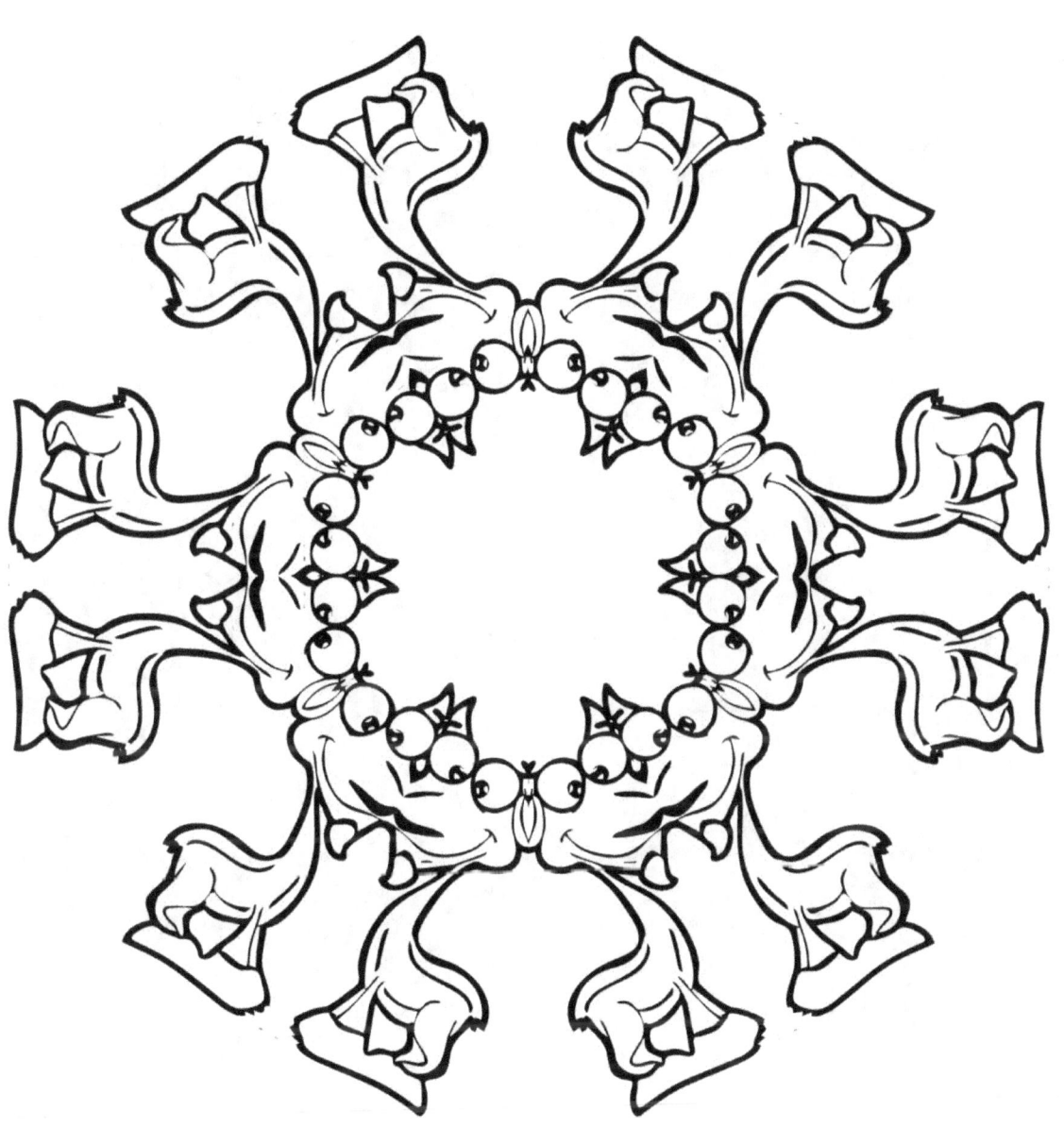

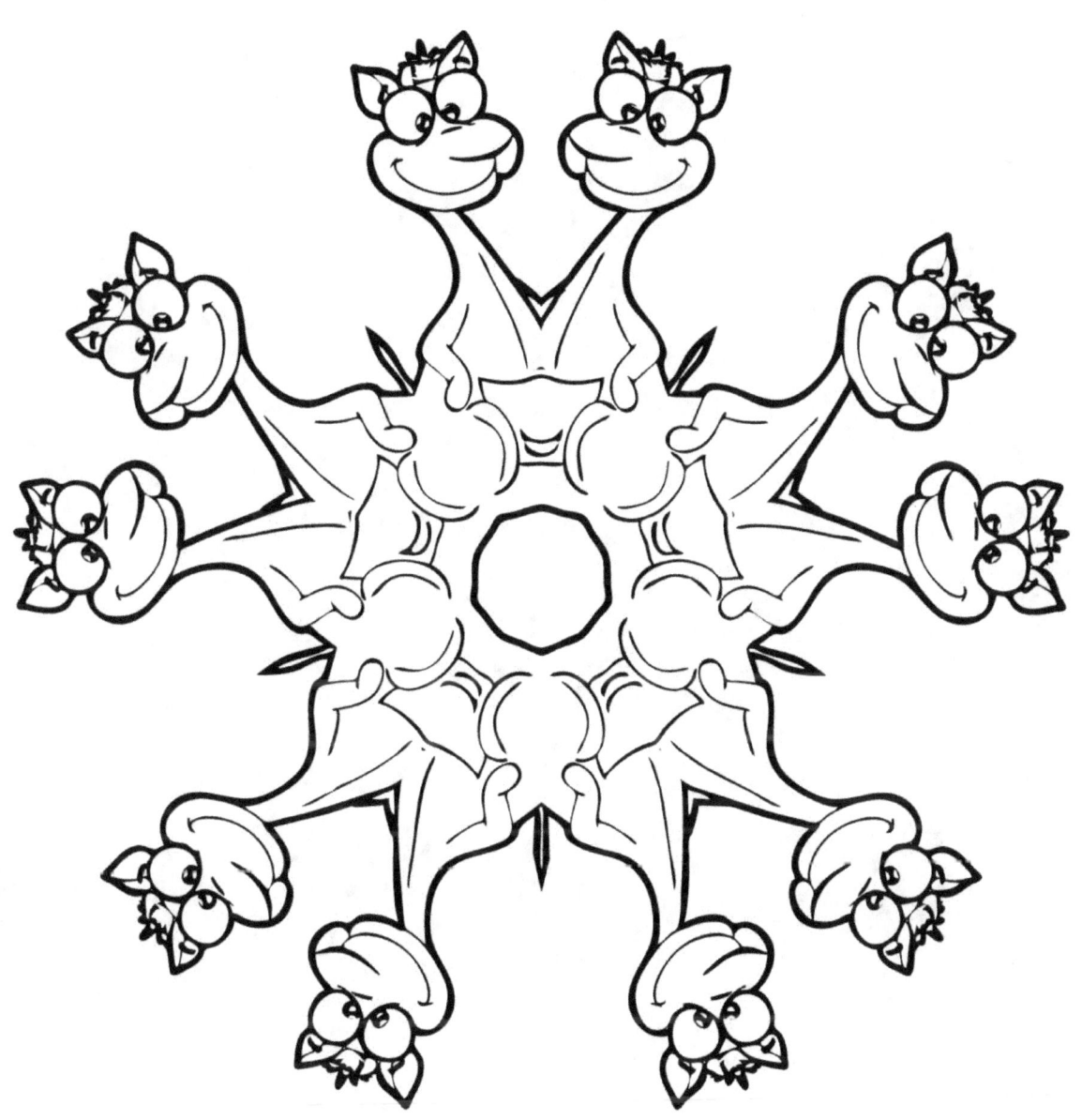

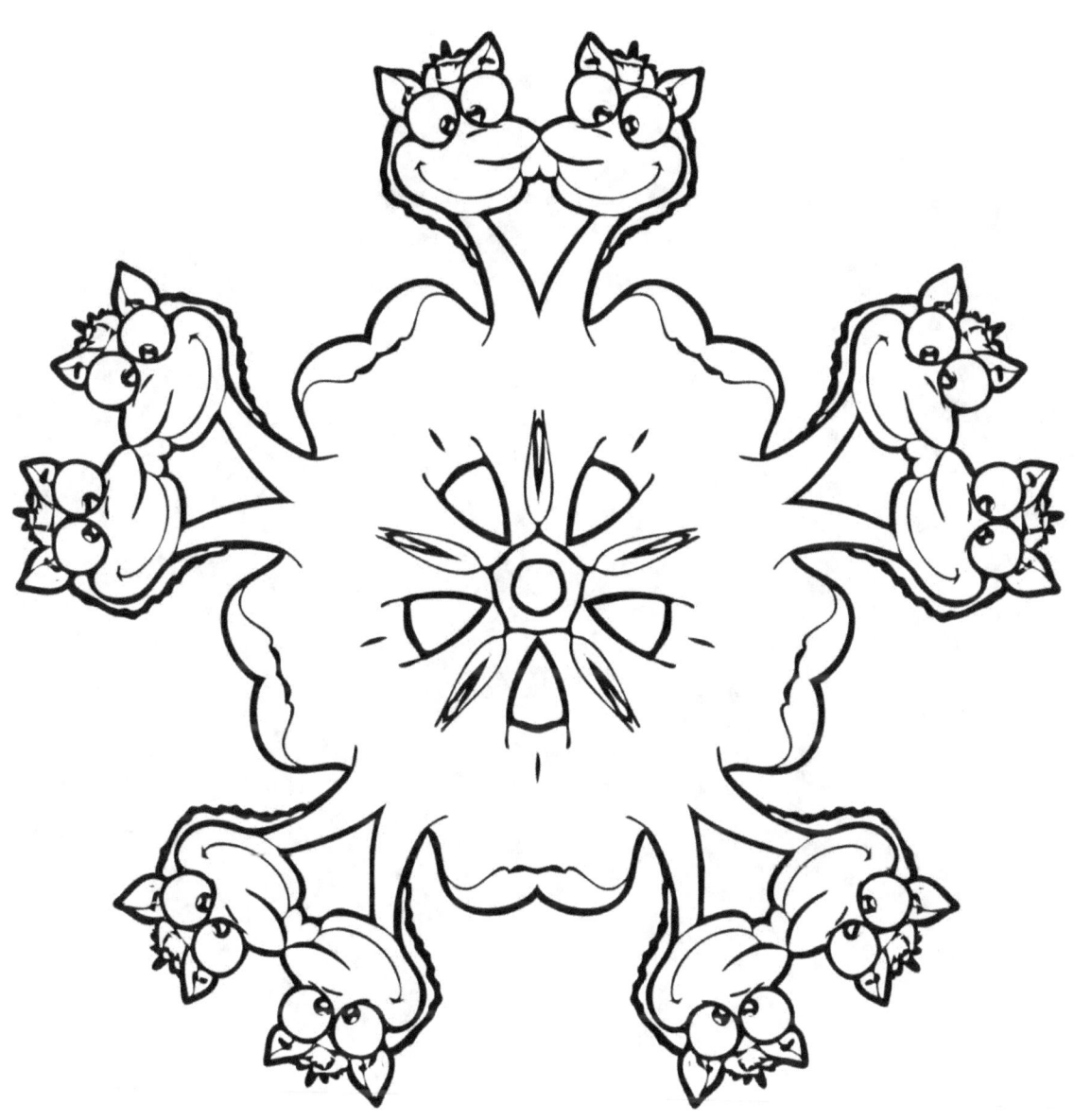

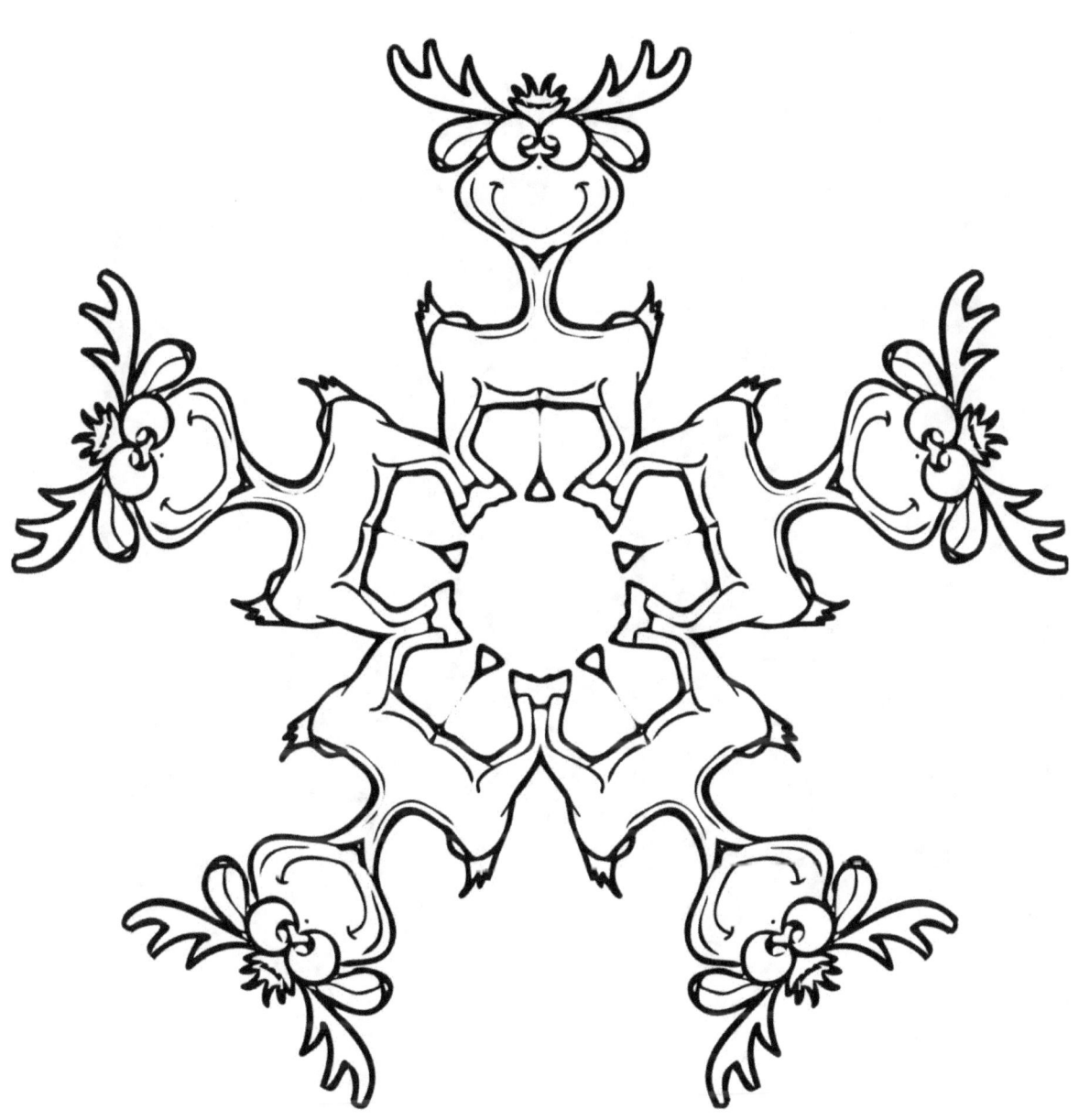

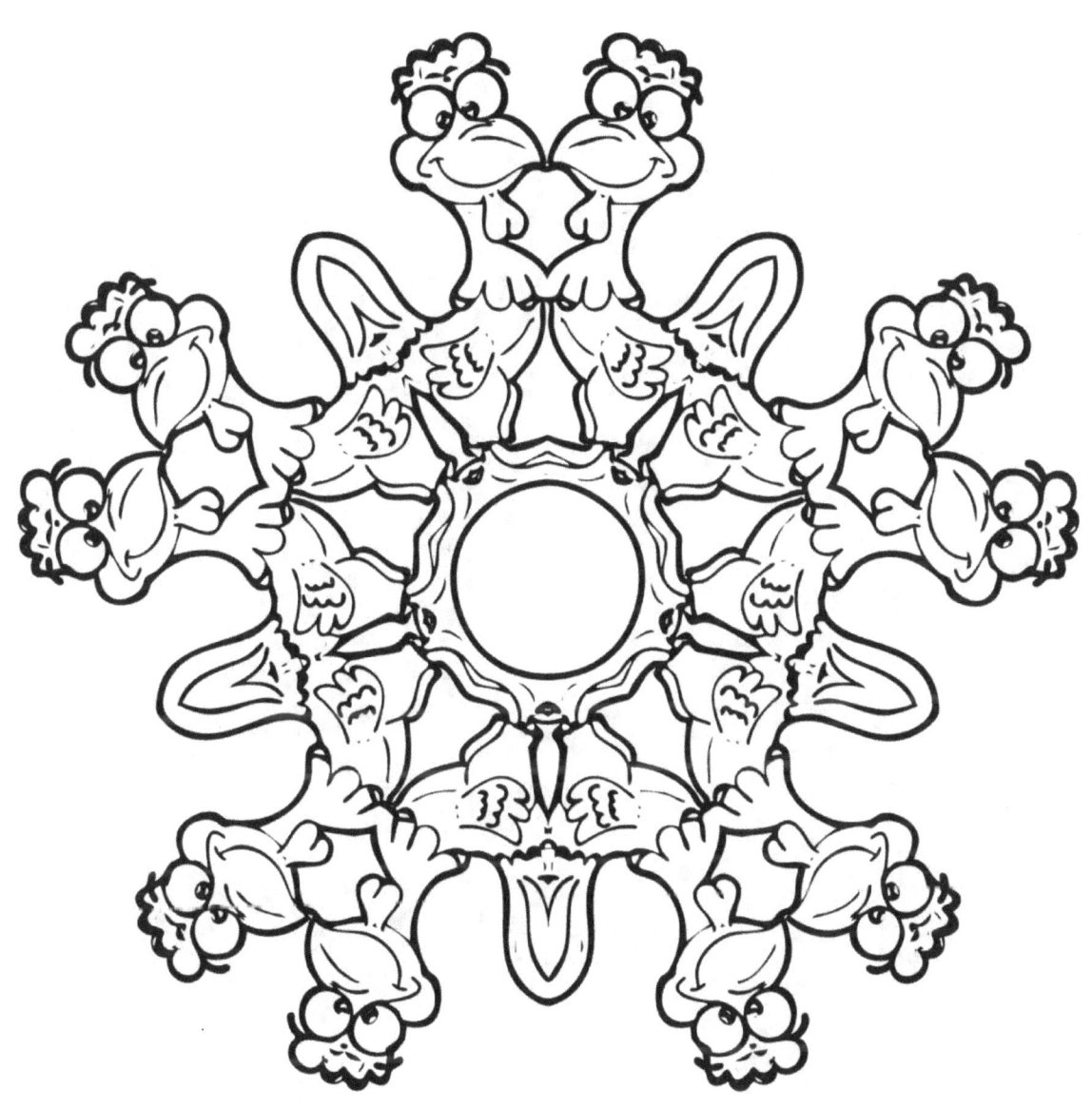

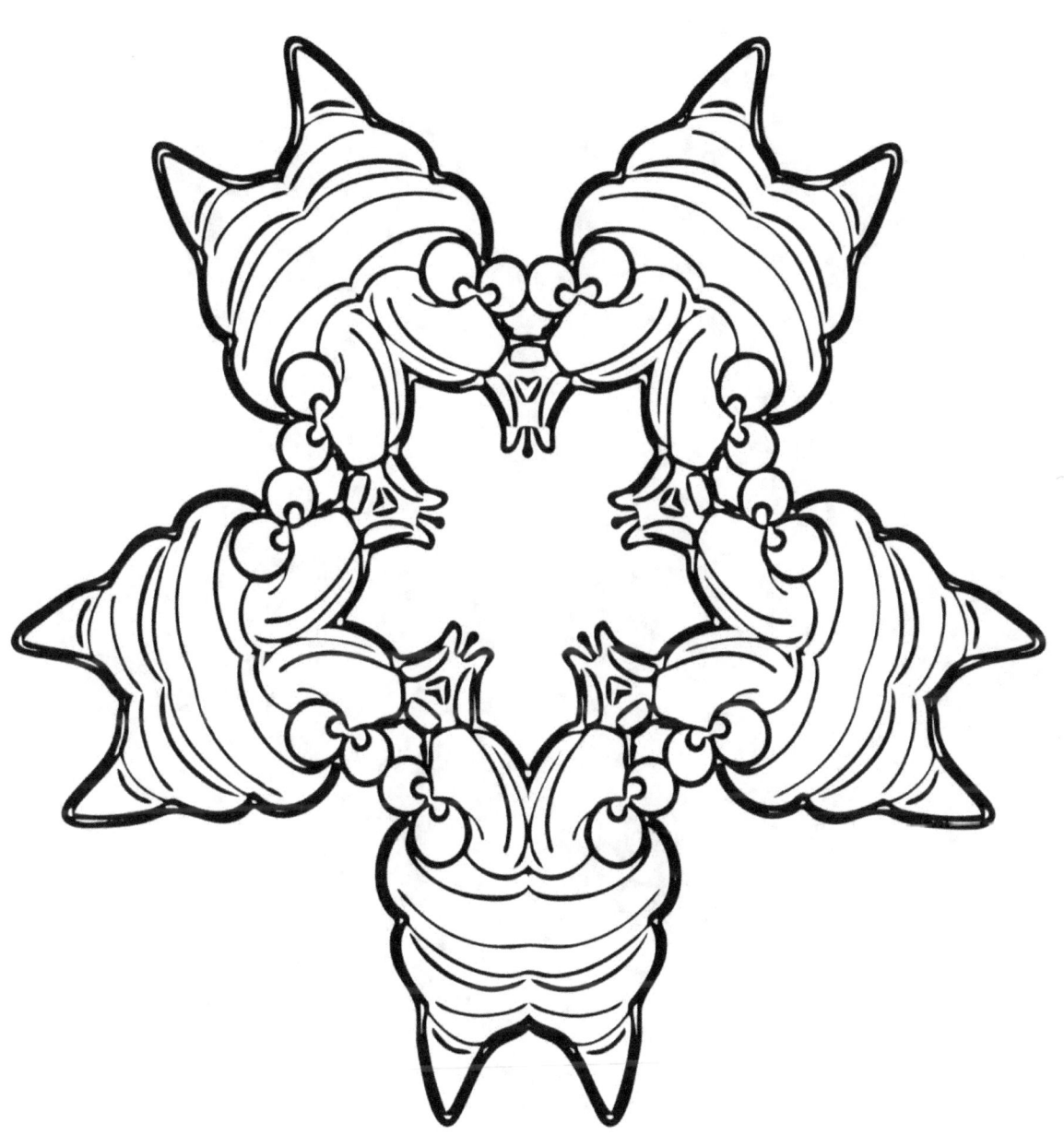

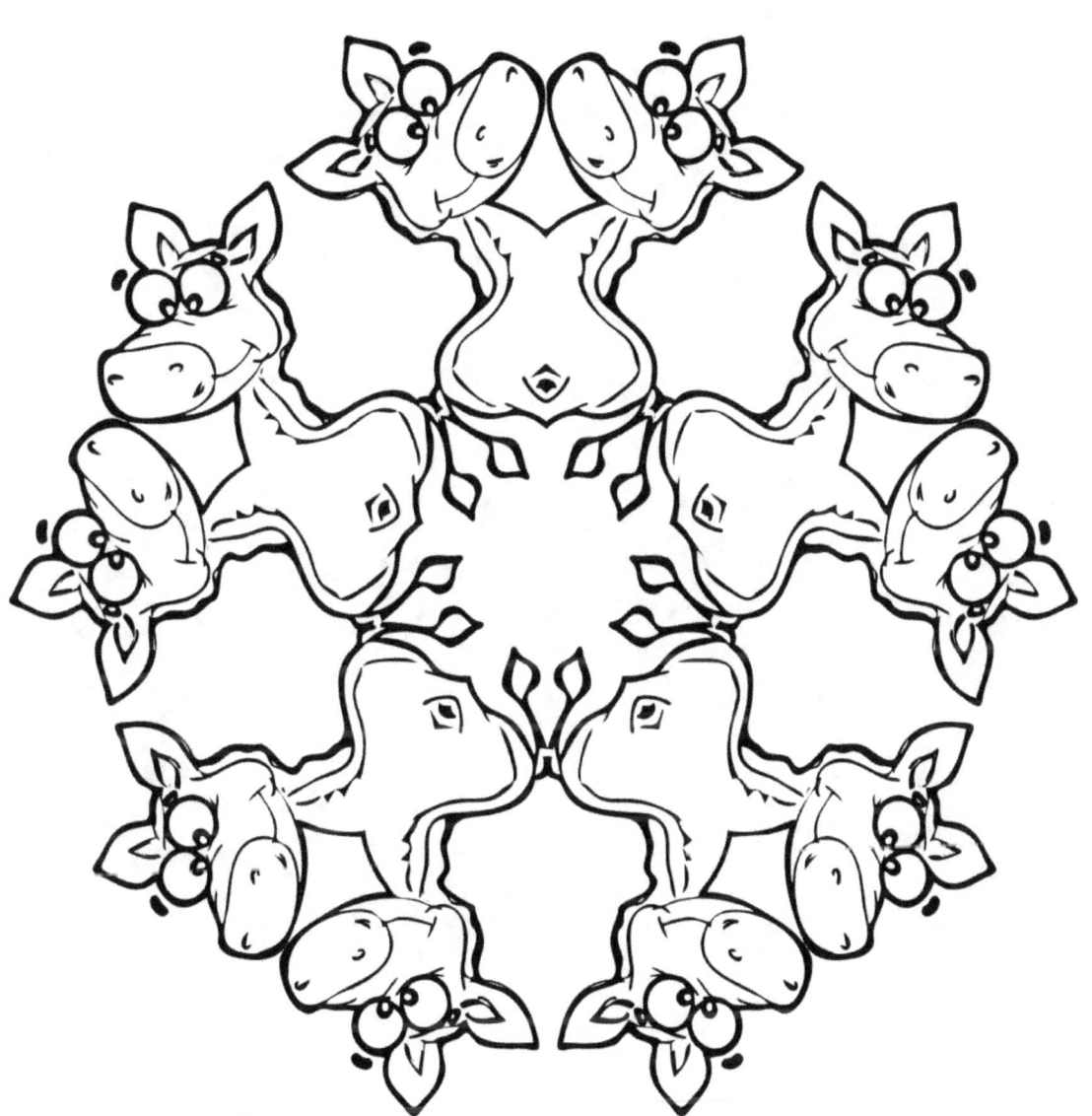

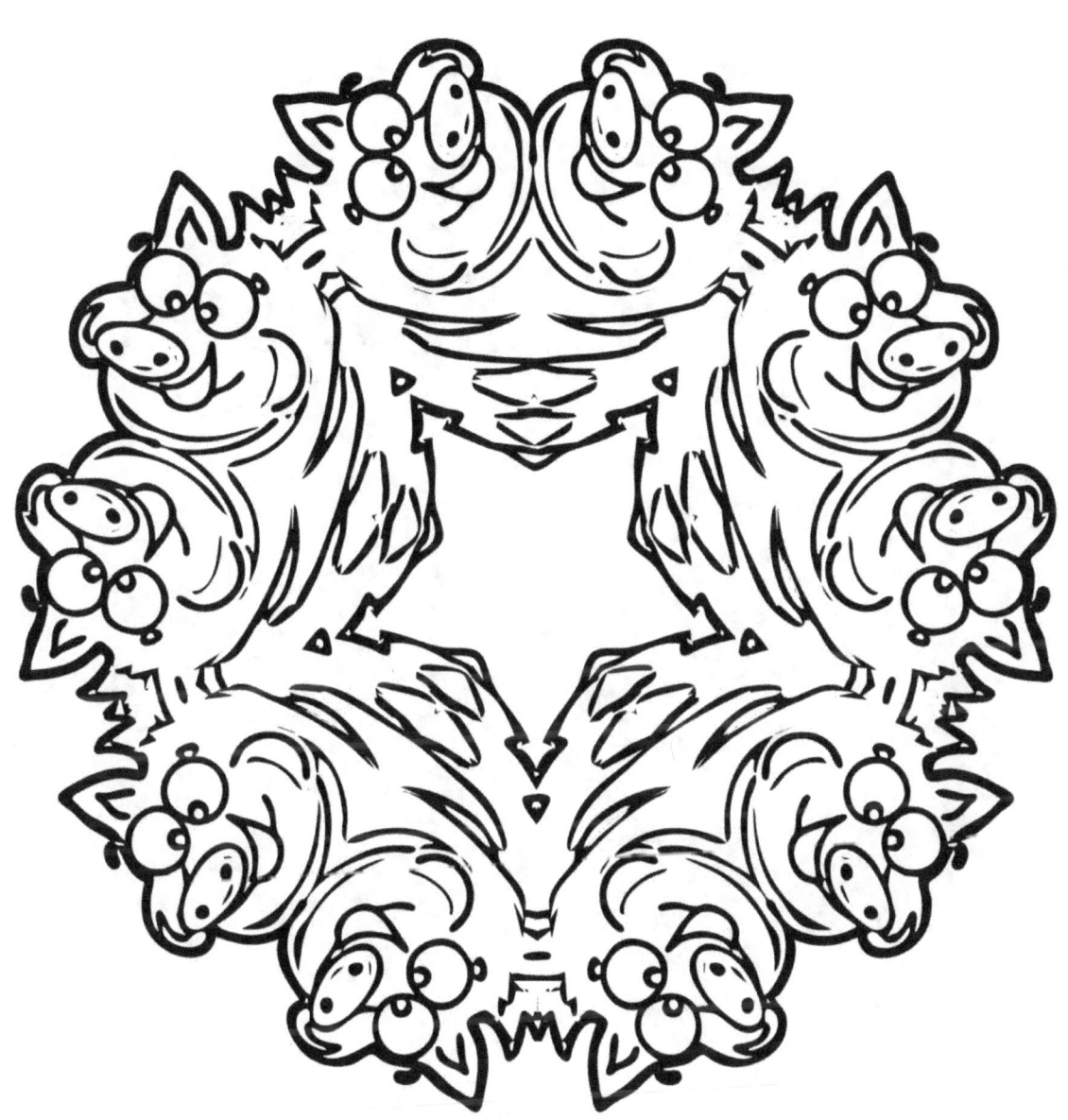

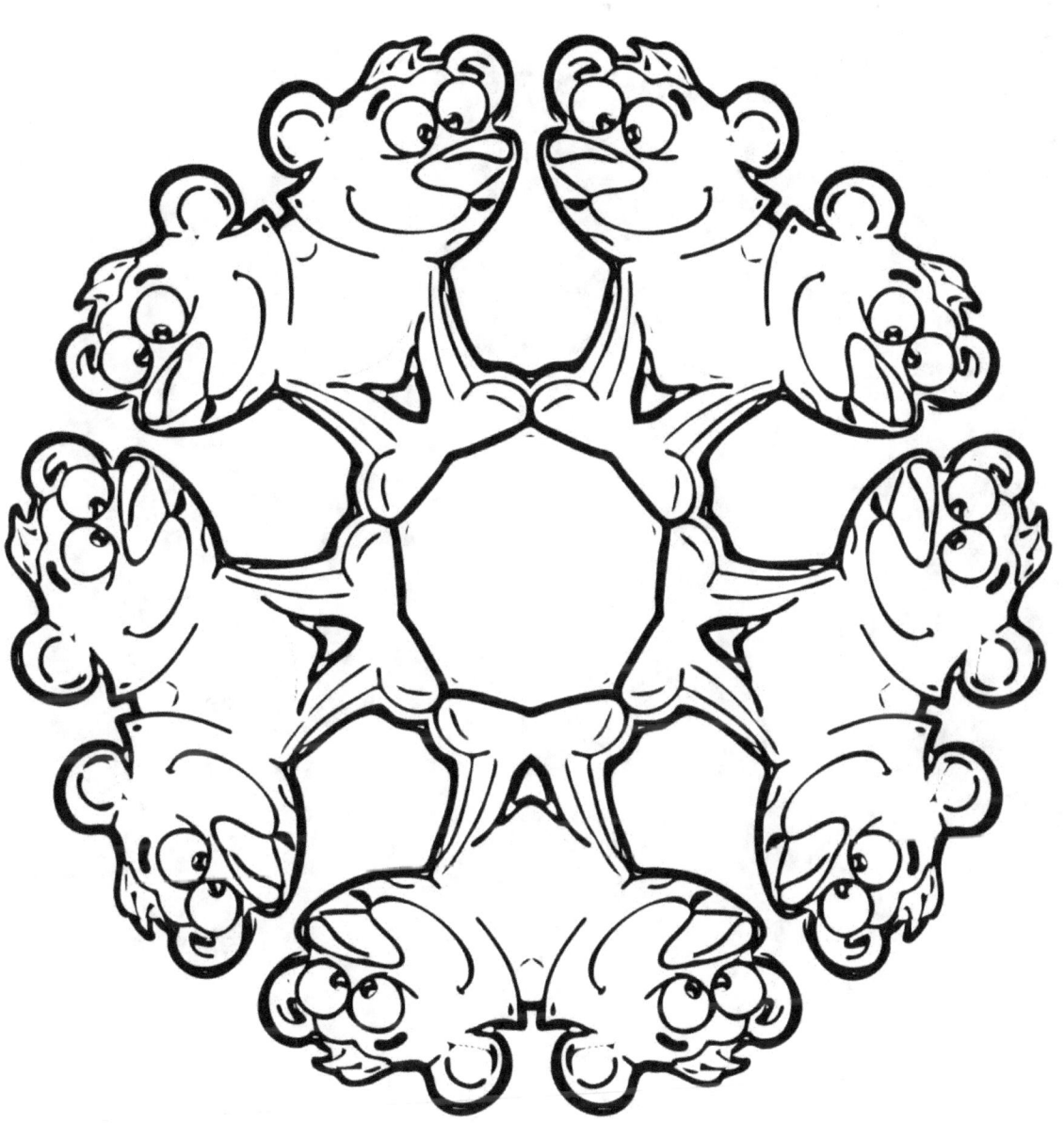

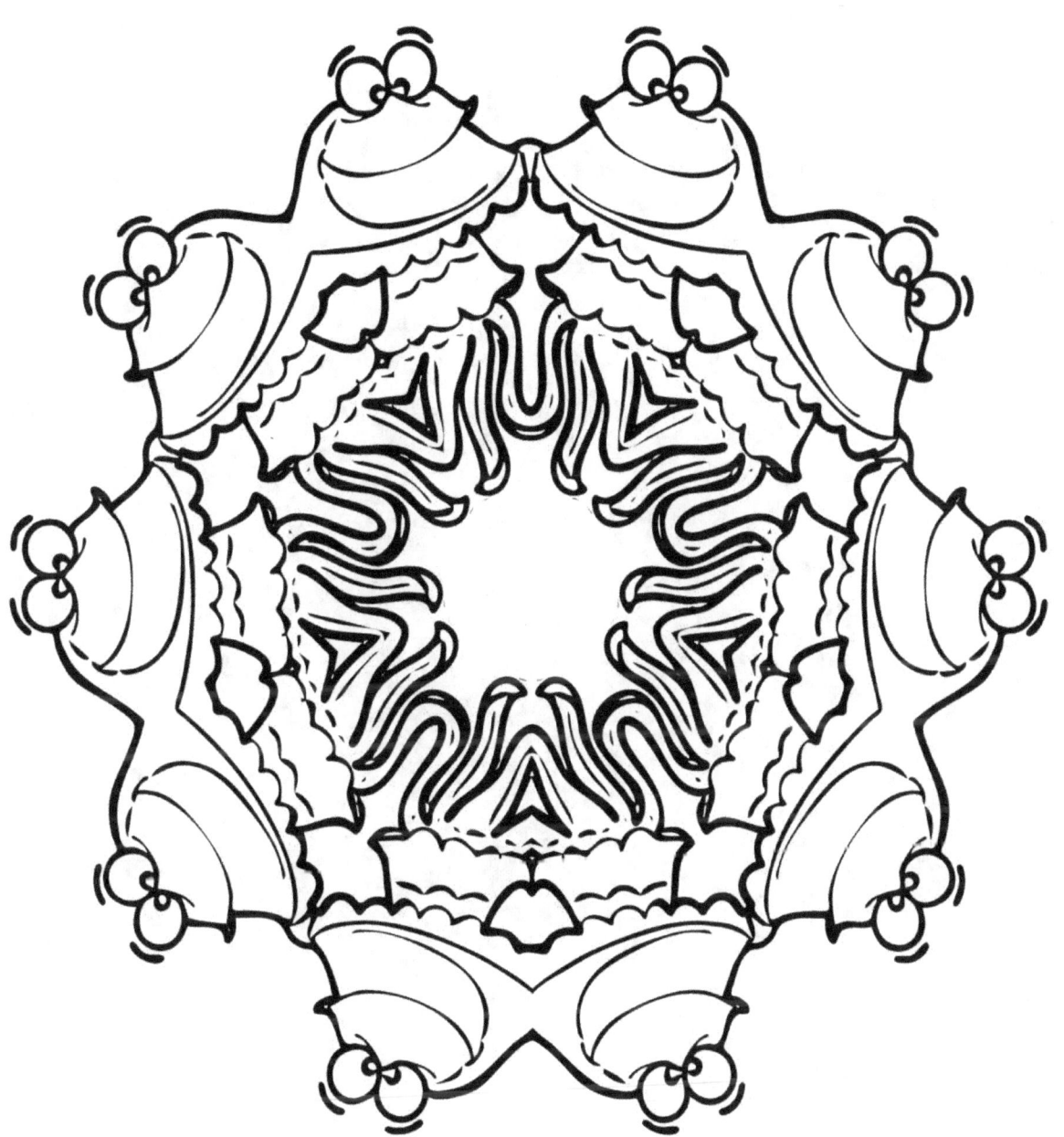

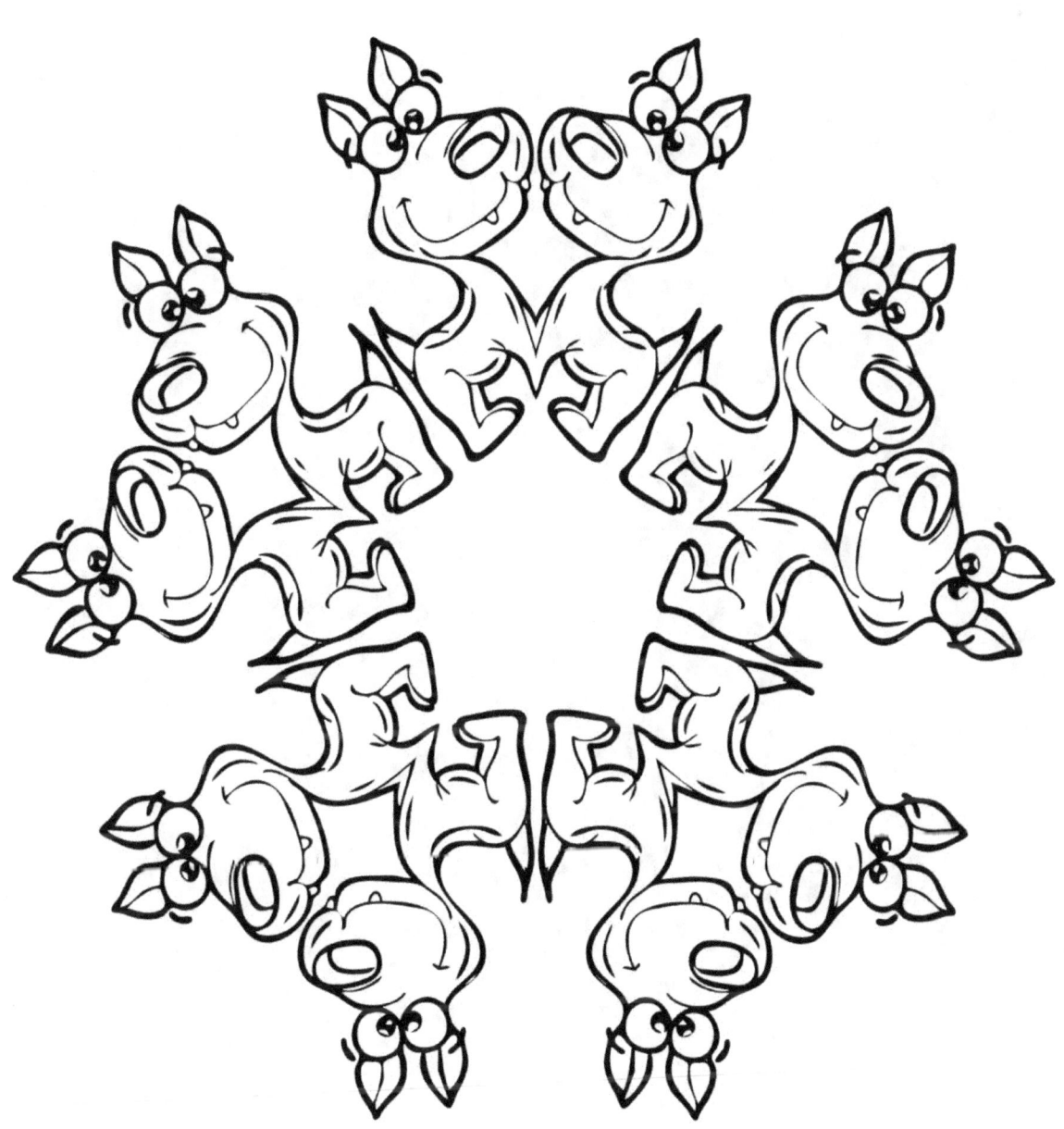

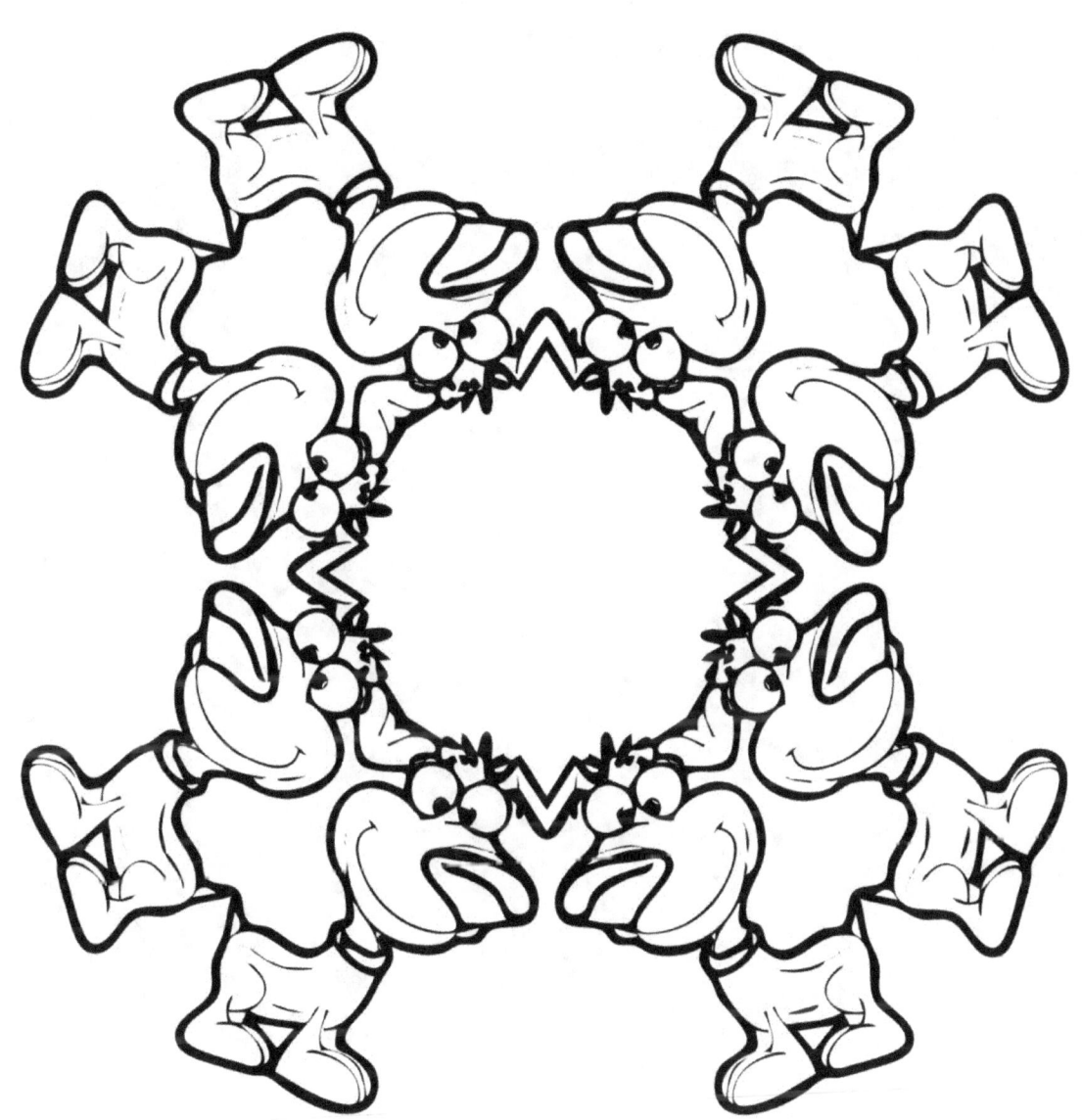

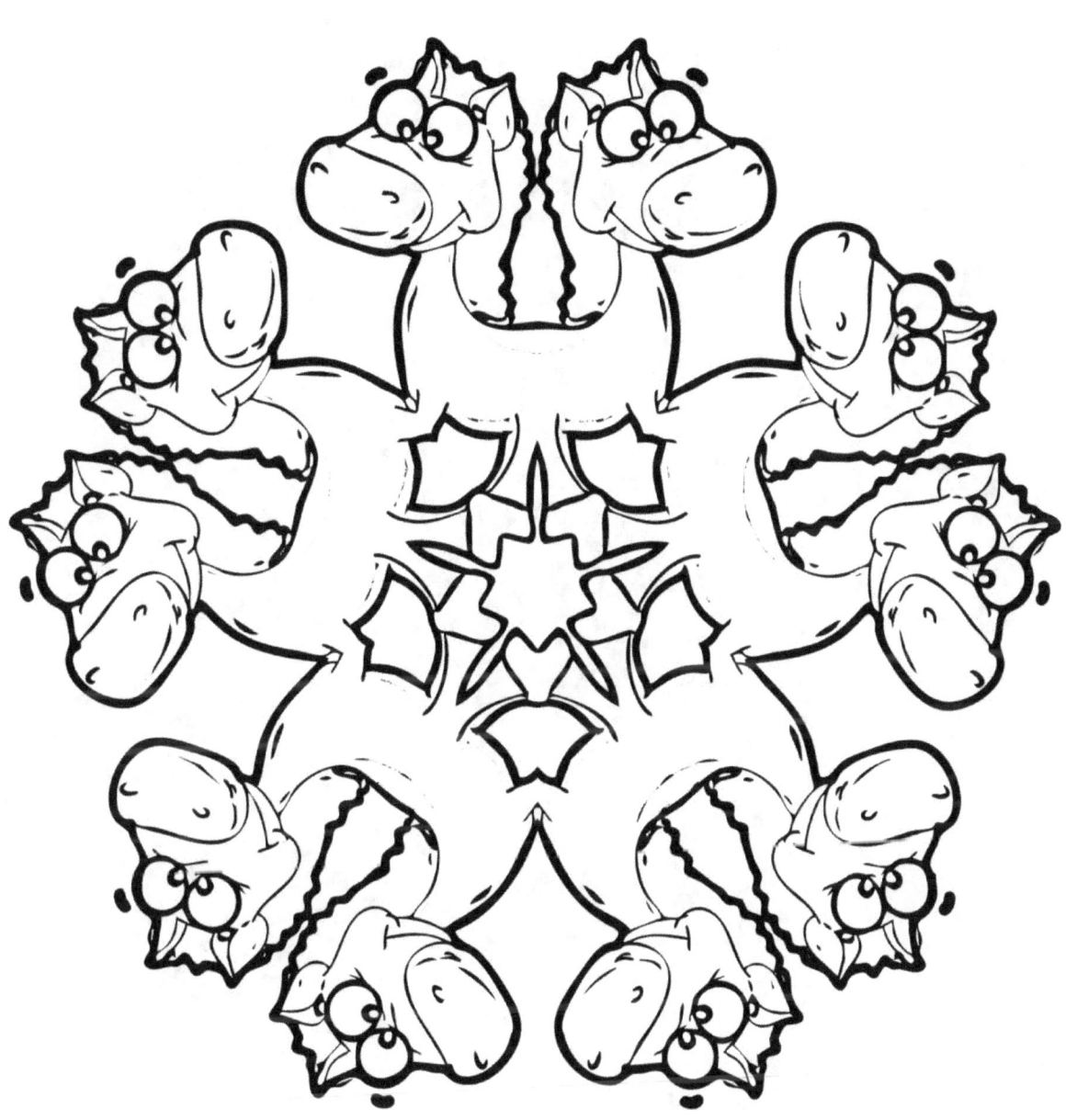

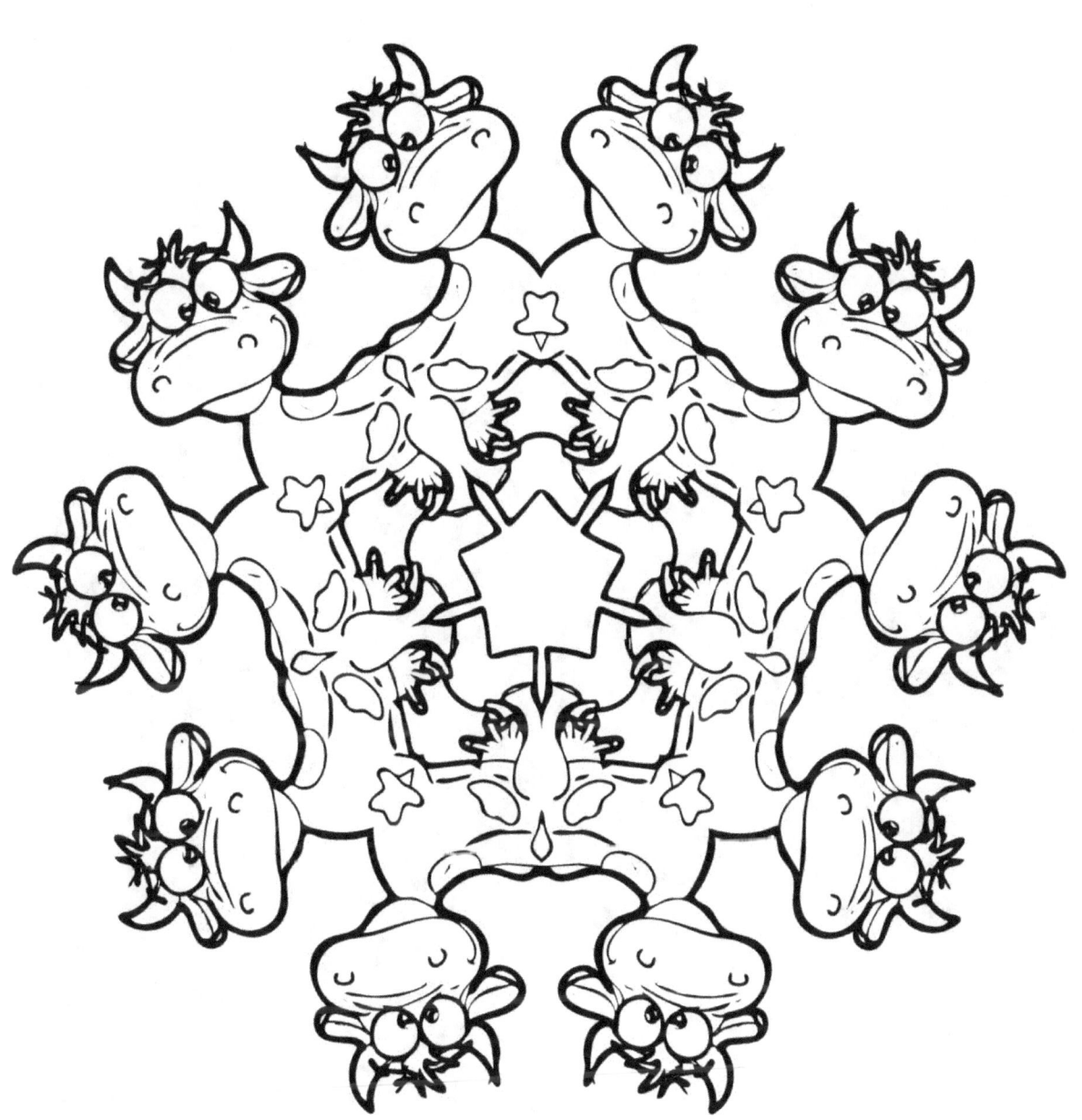

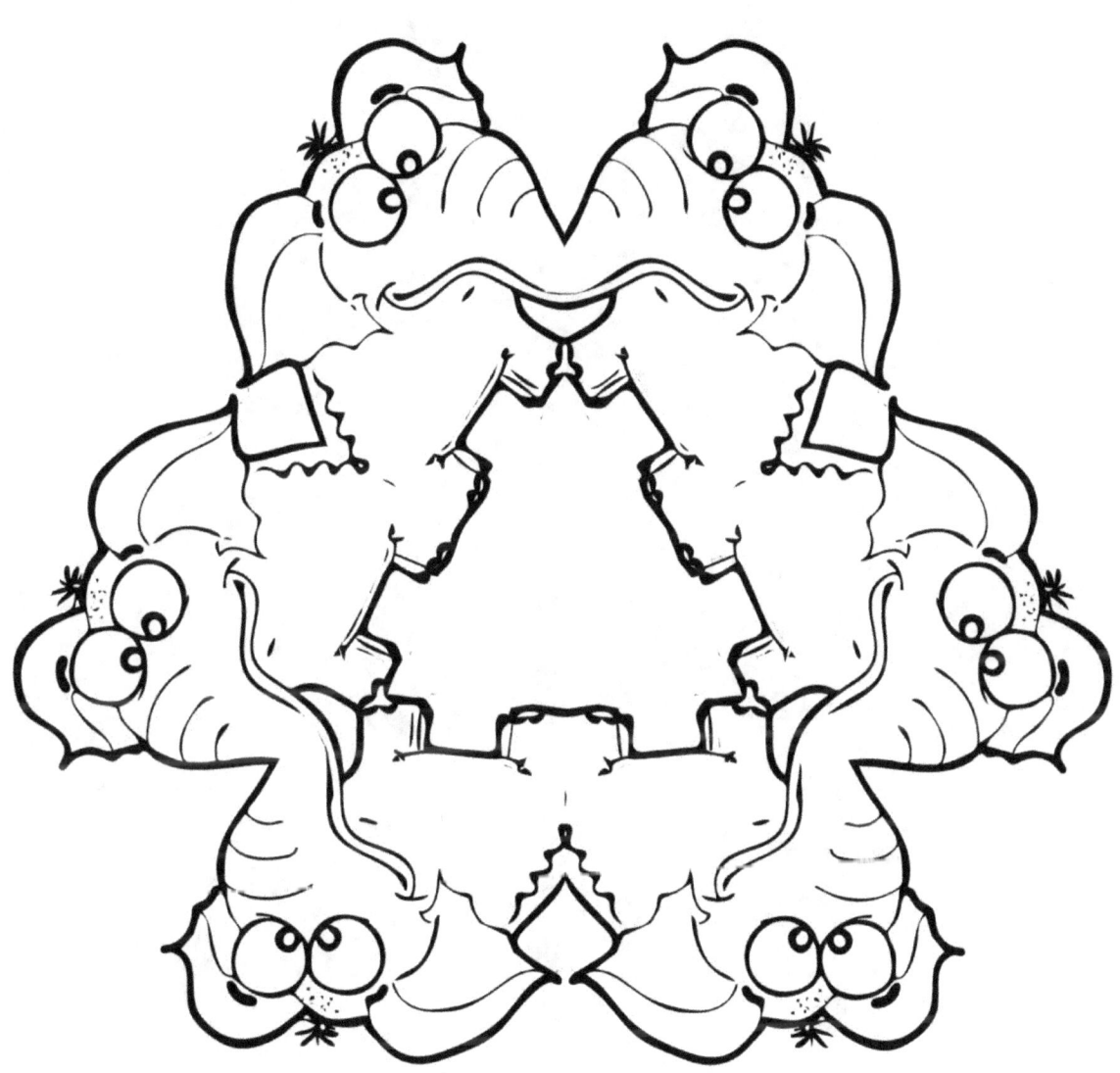

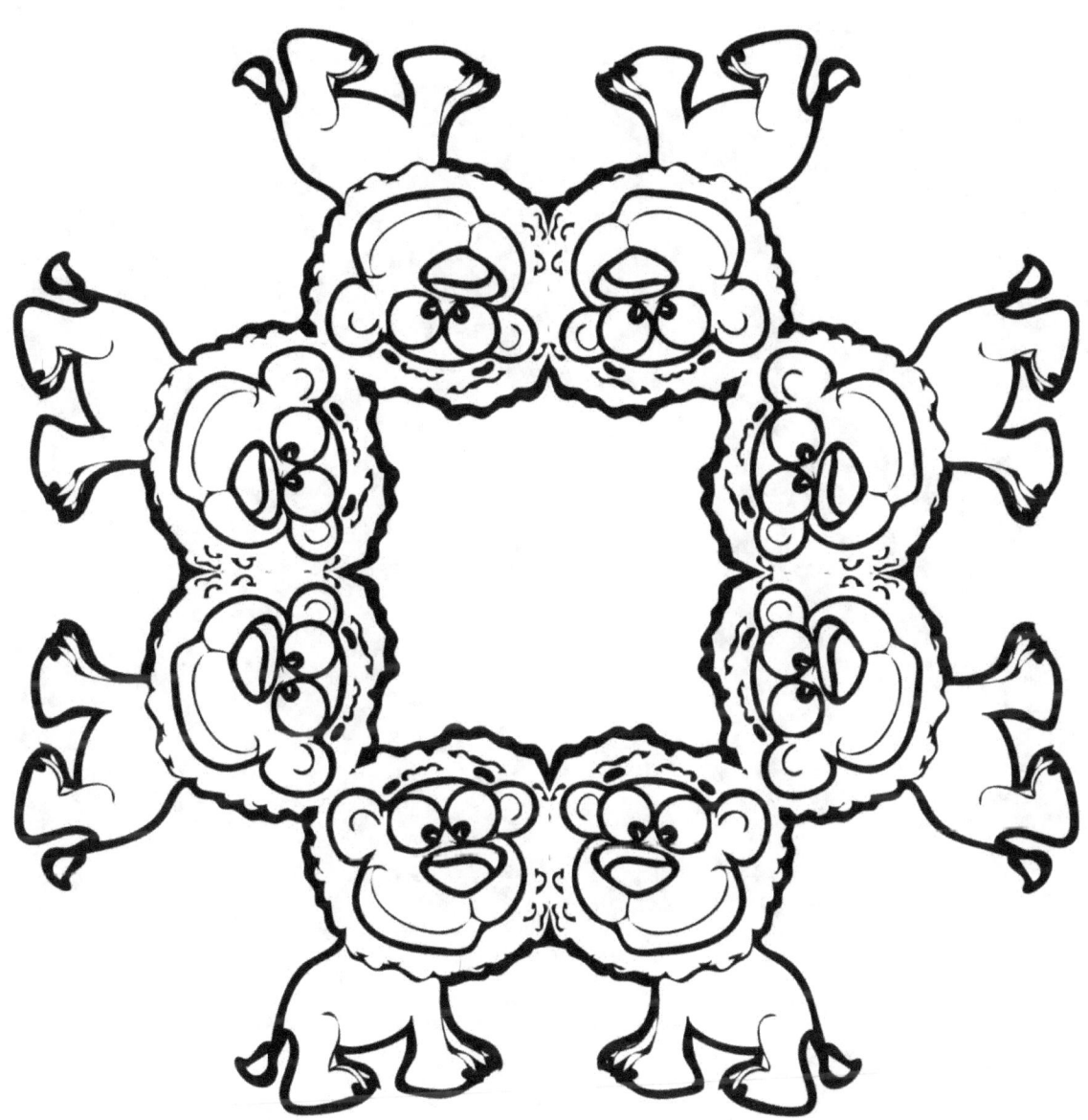

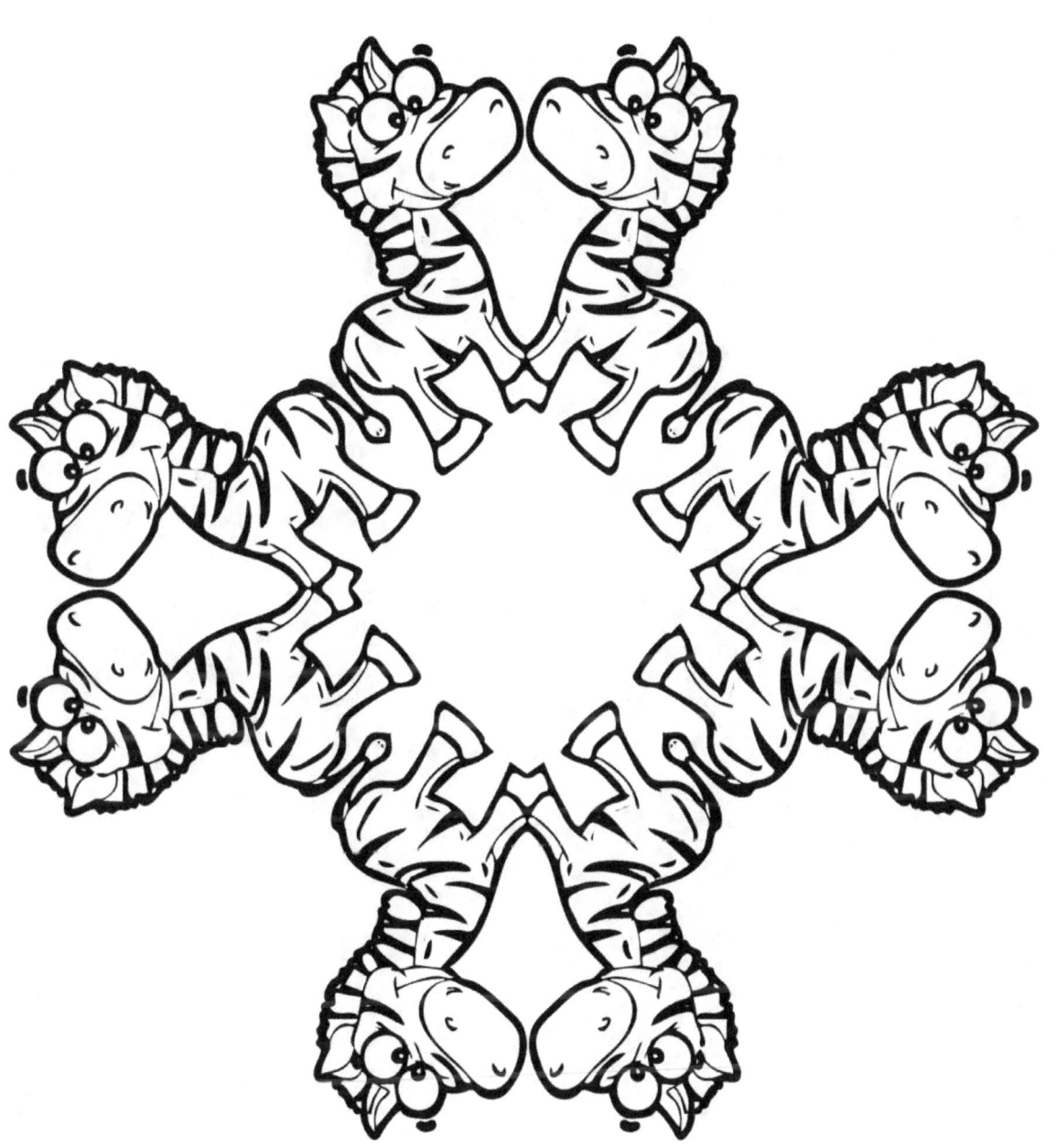

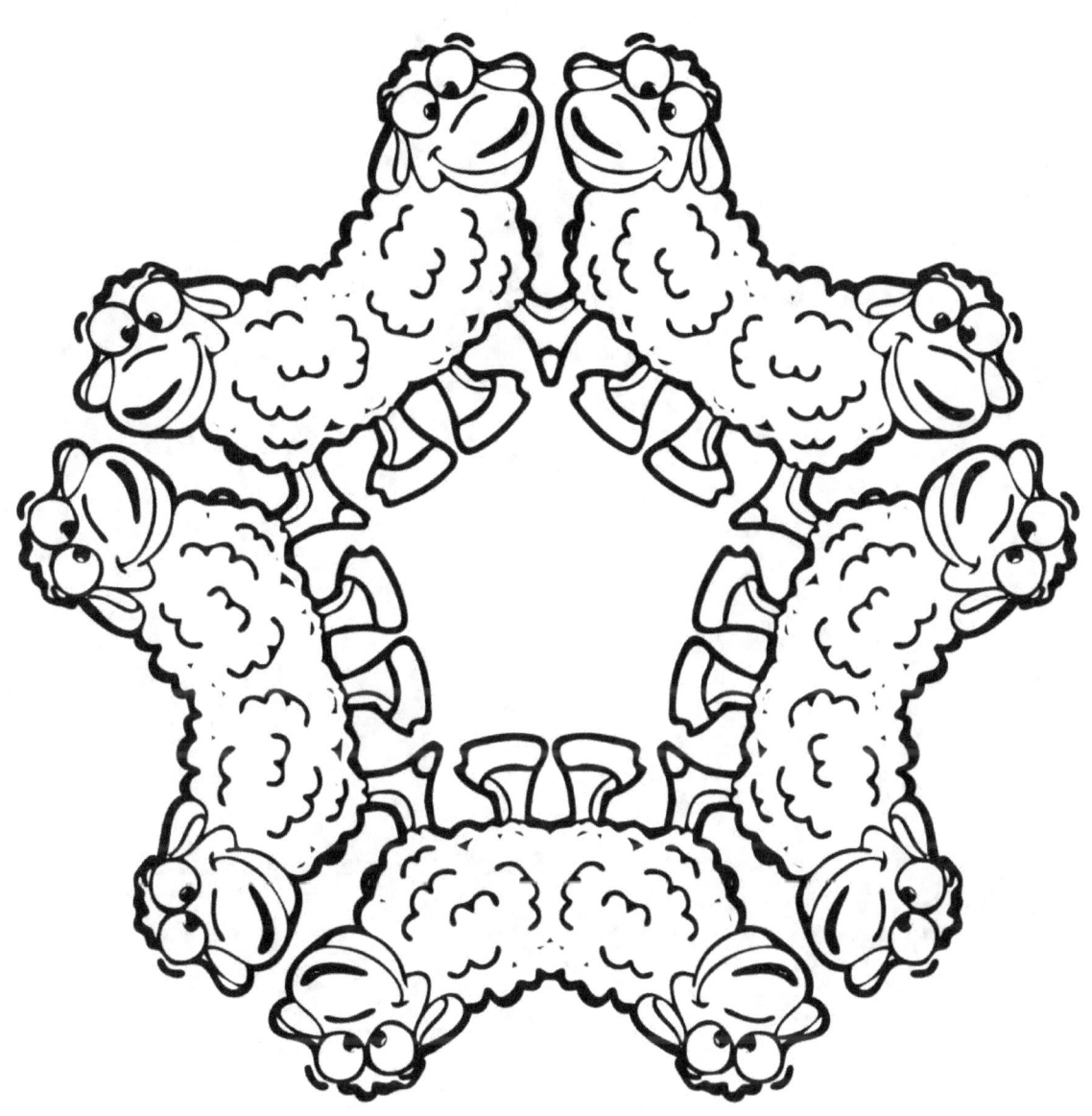

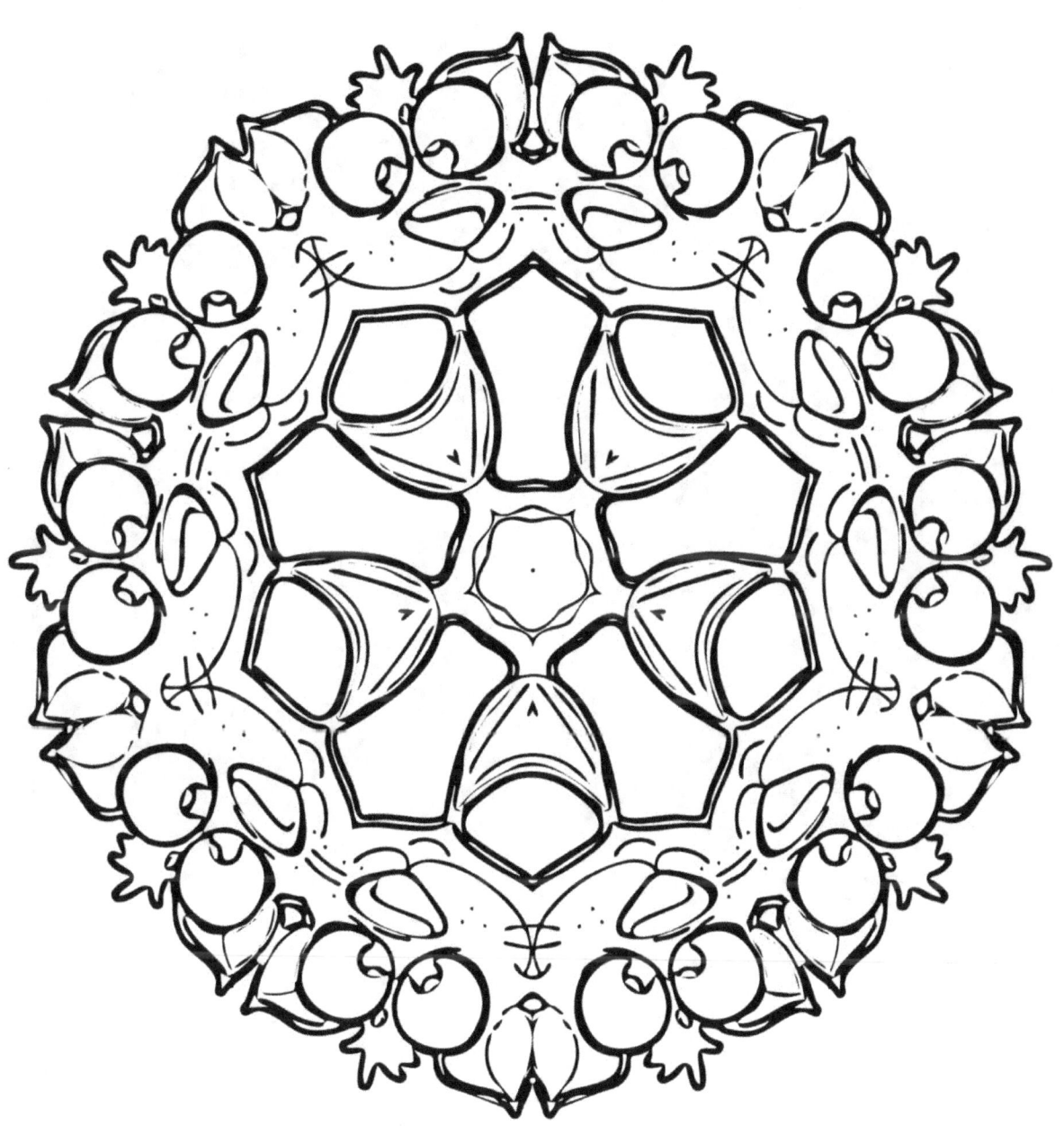

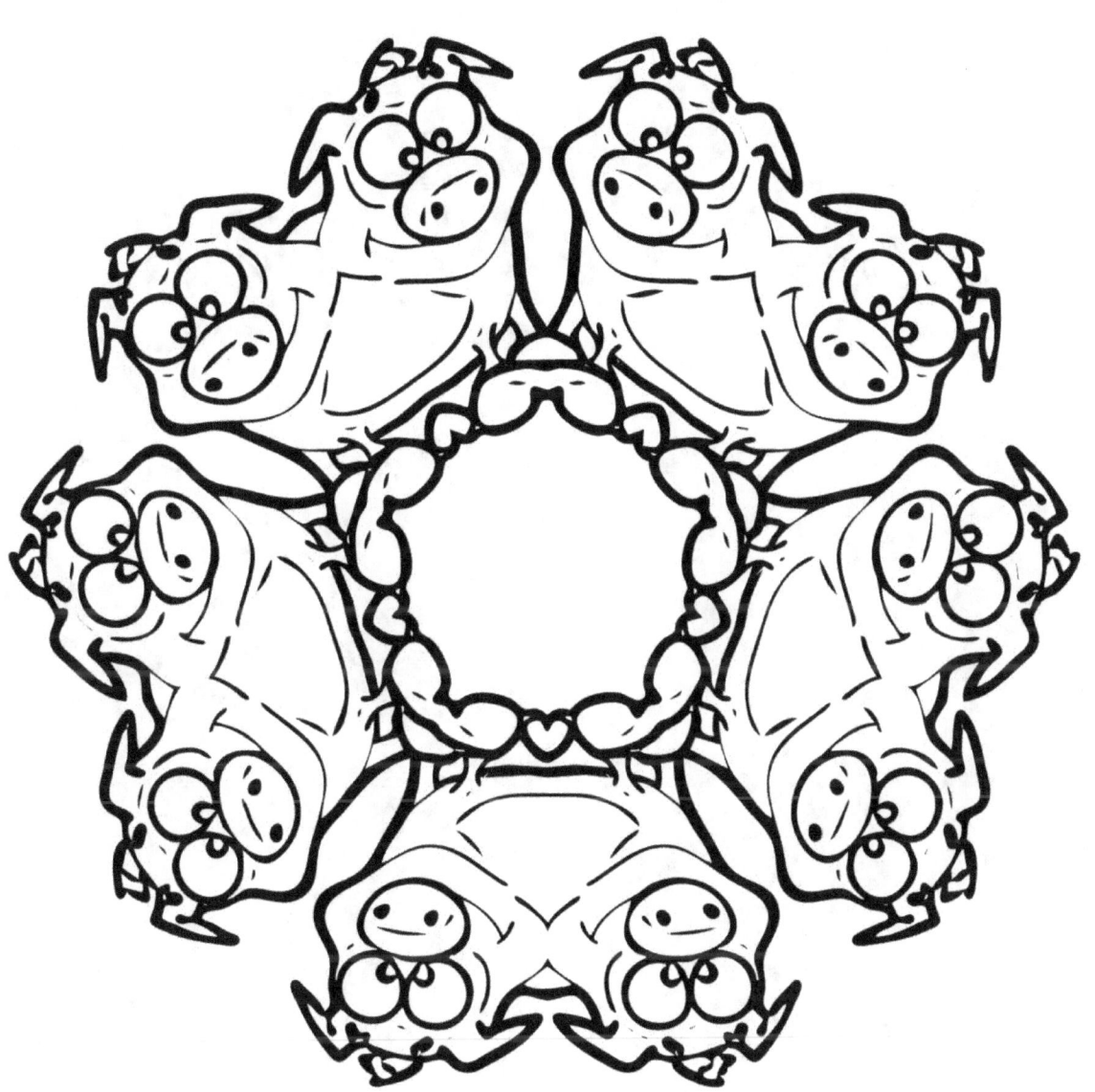

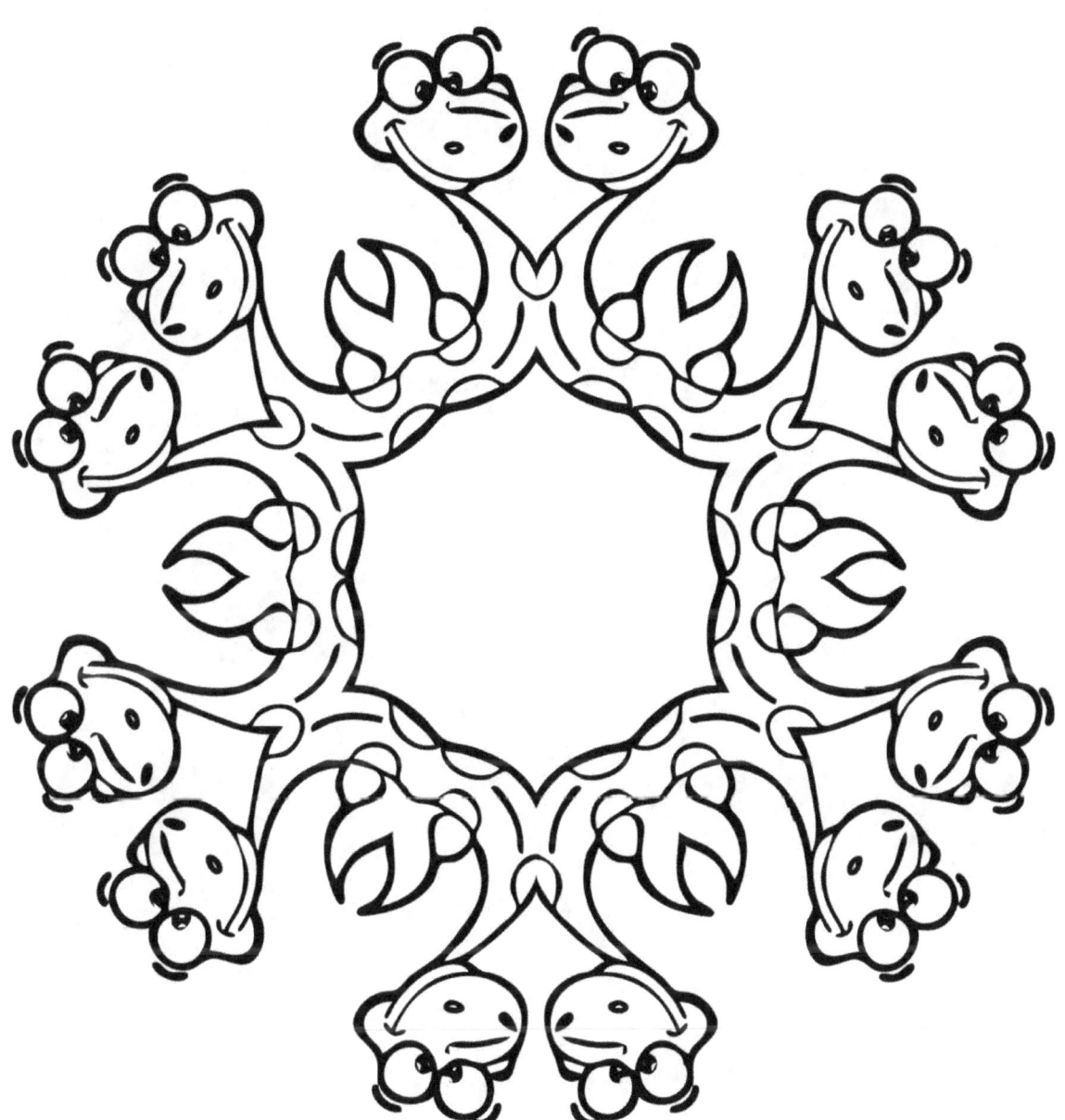

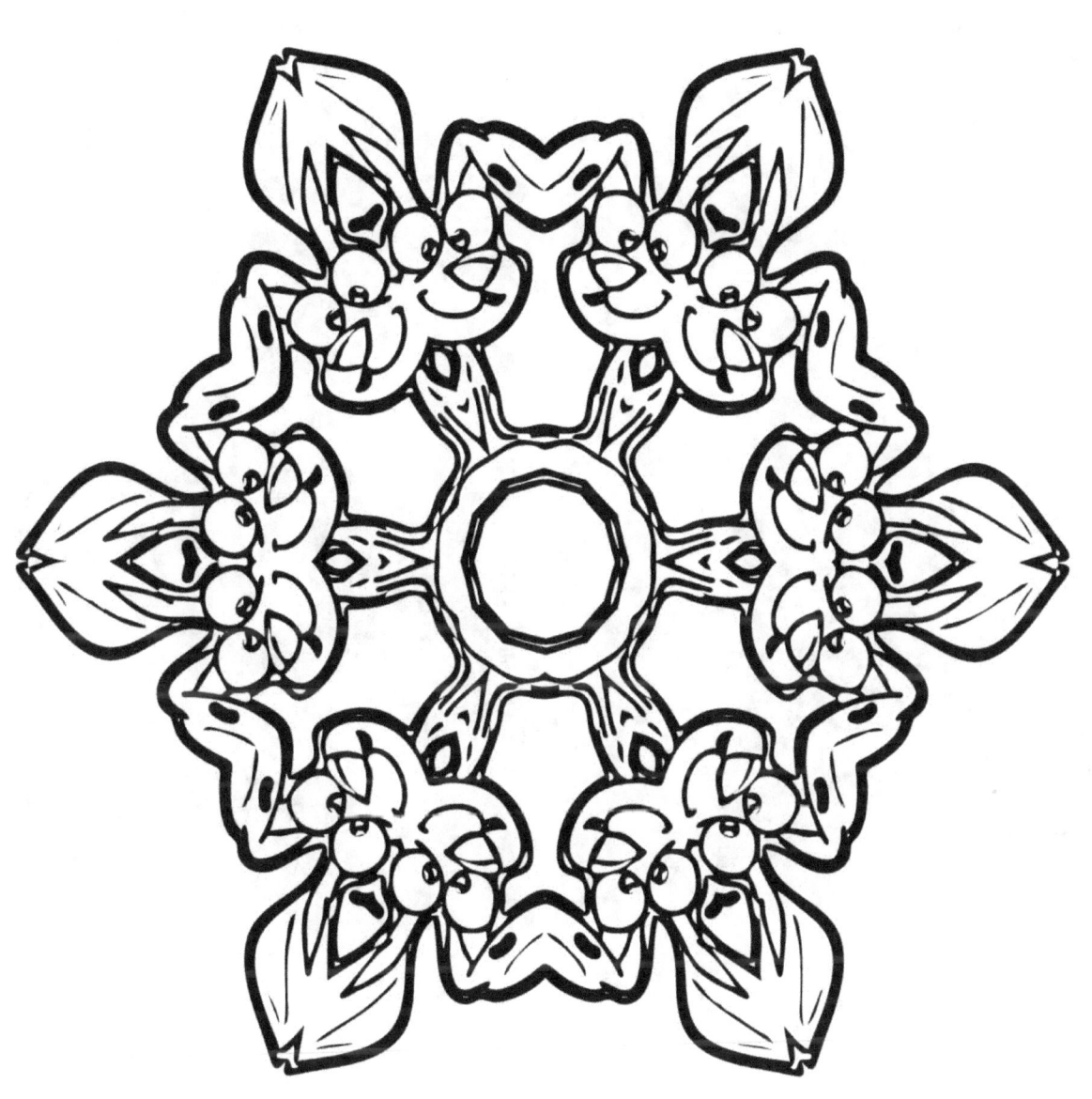

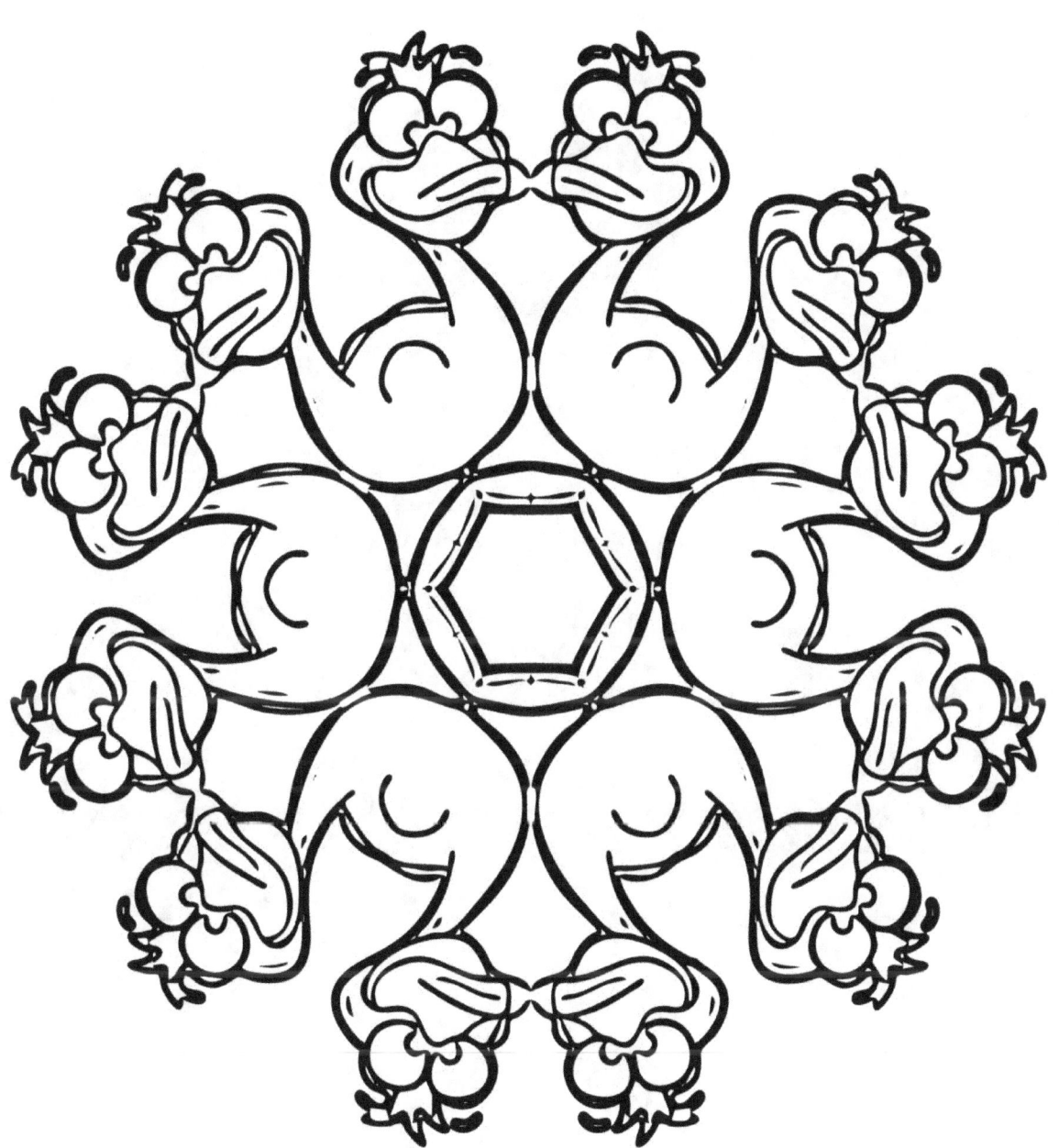

Animals Coloring Book
PSYCHEDELIC
STRESS-RELIEVING ANIMALS
2
A Coloring Book For Adults

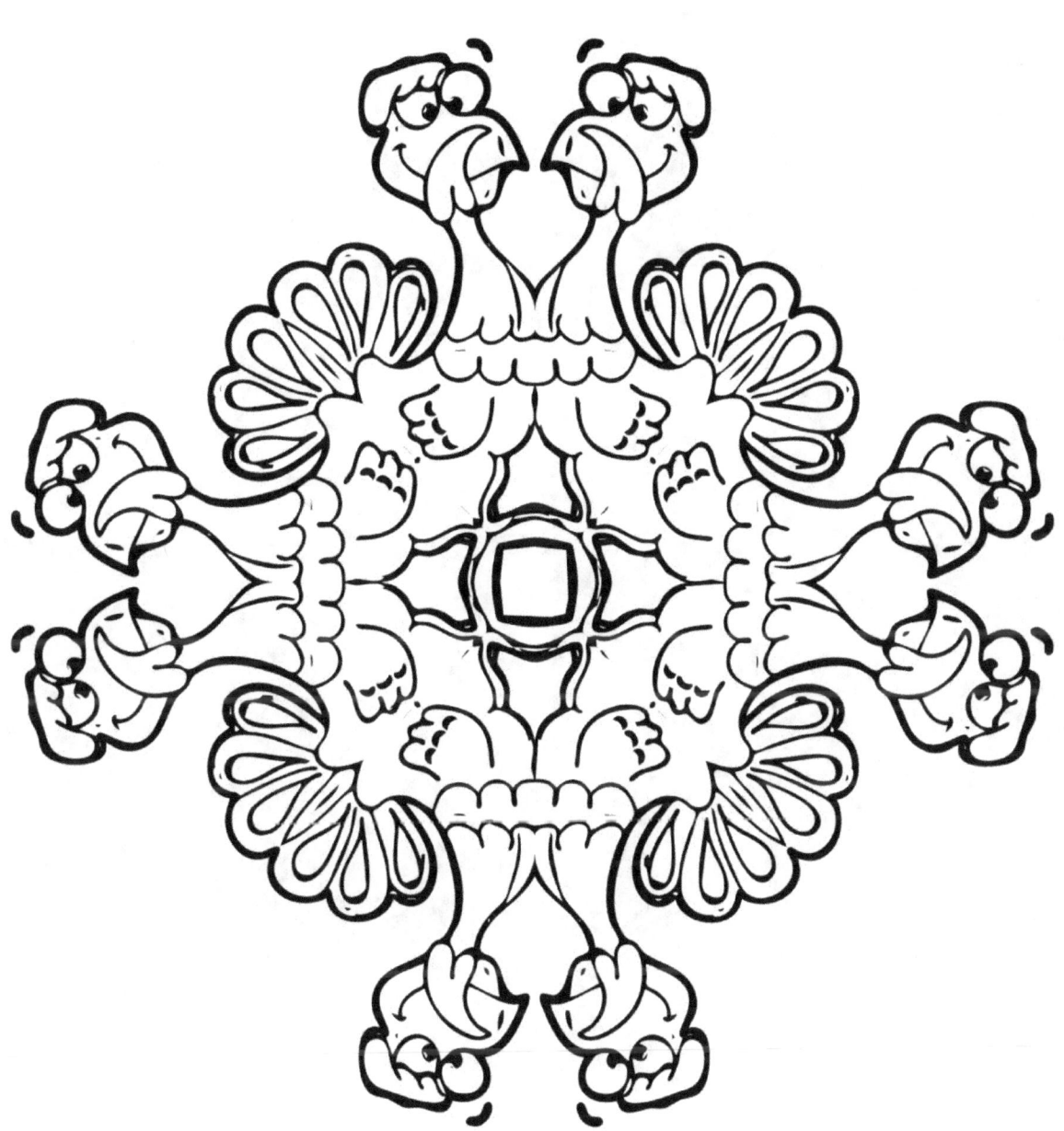

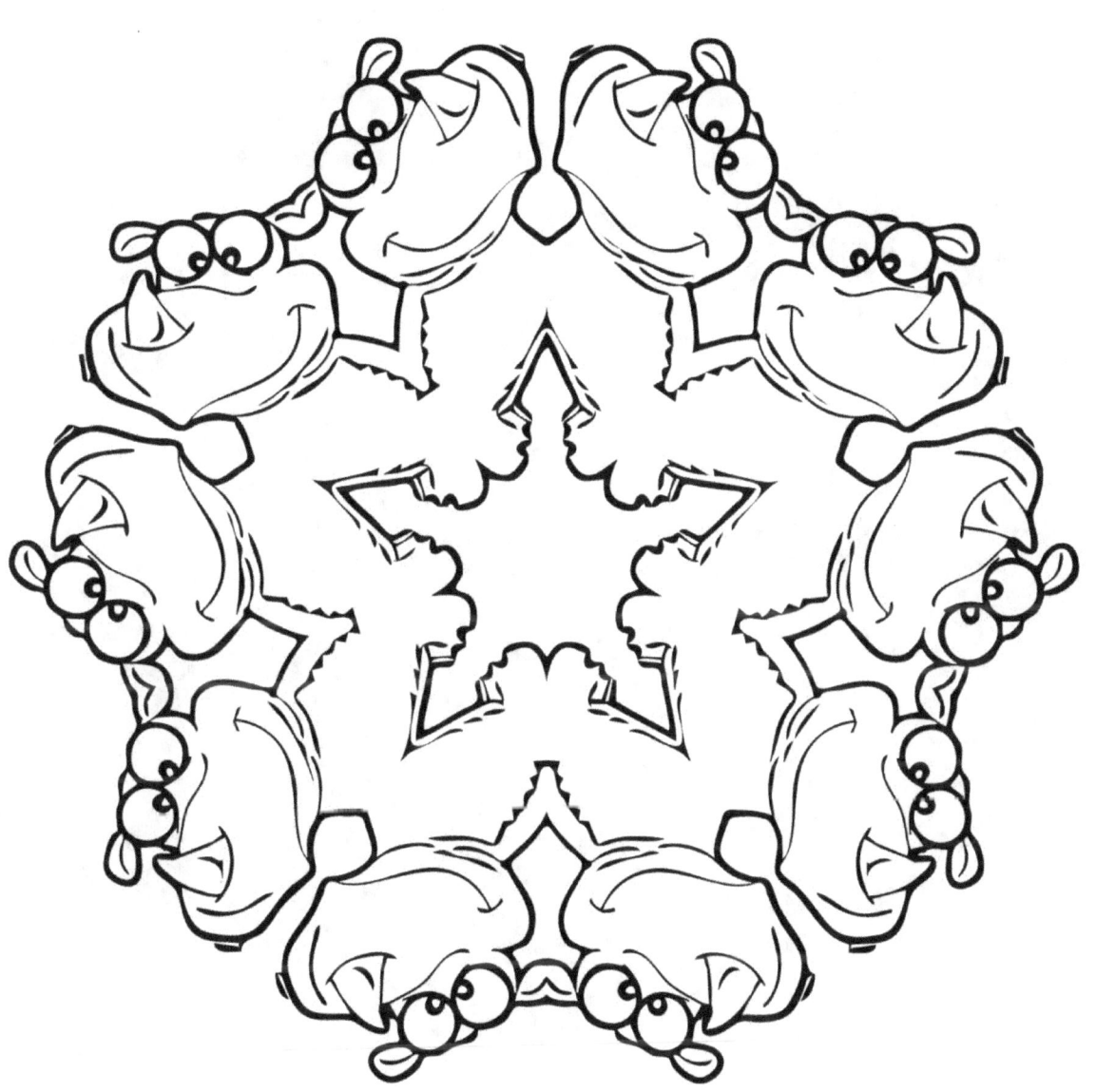

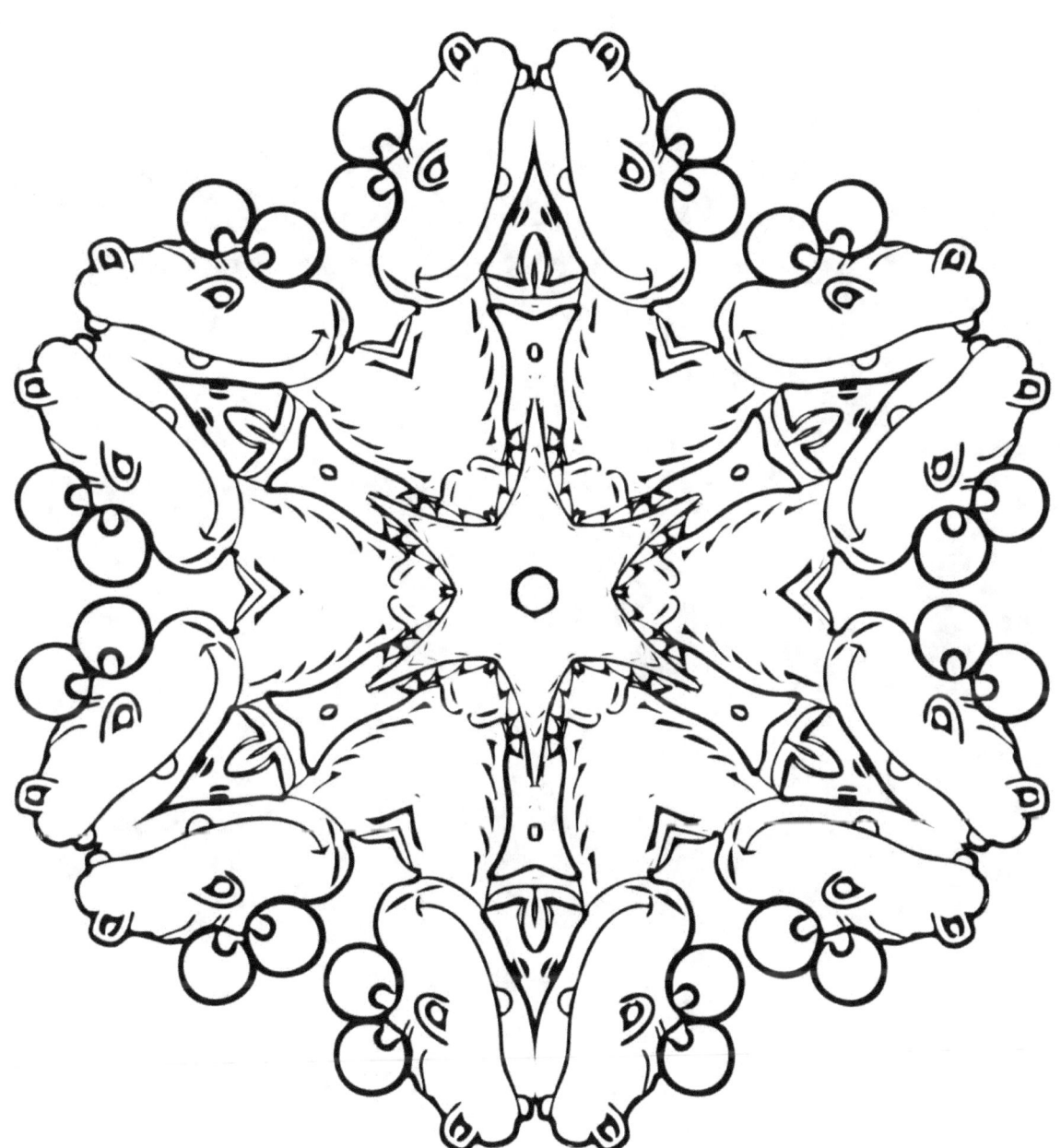

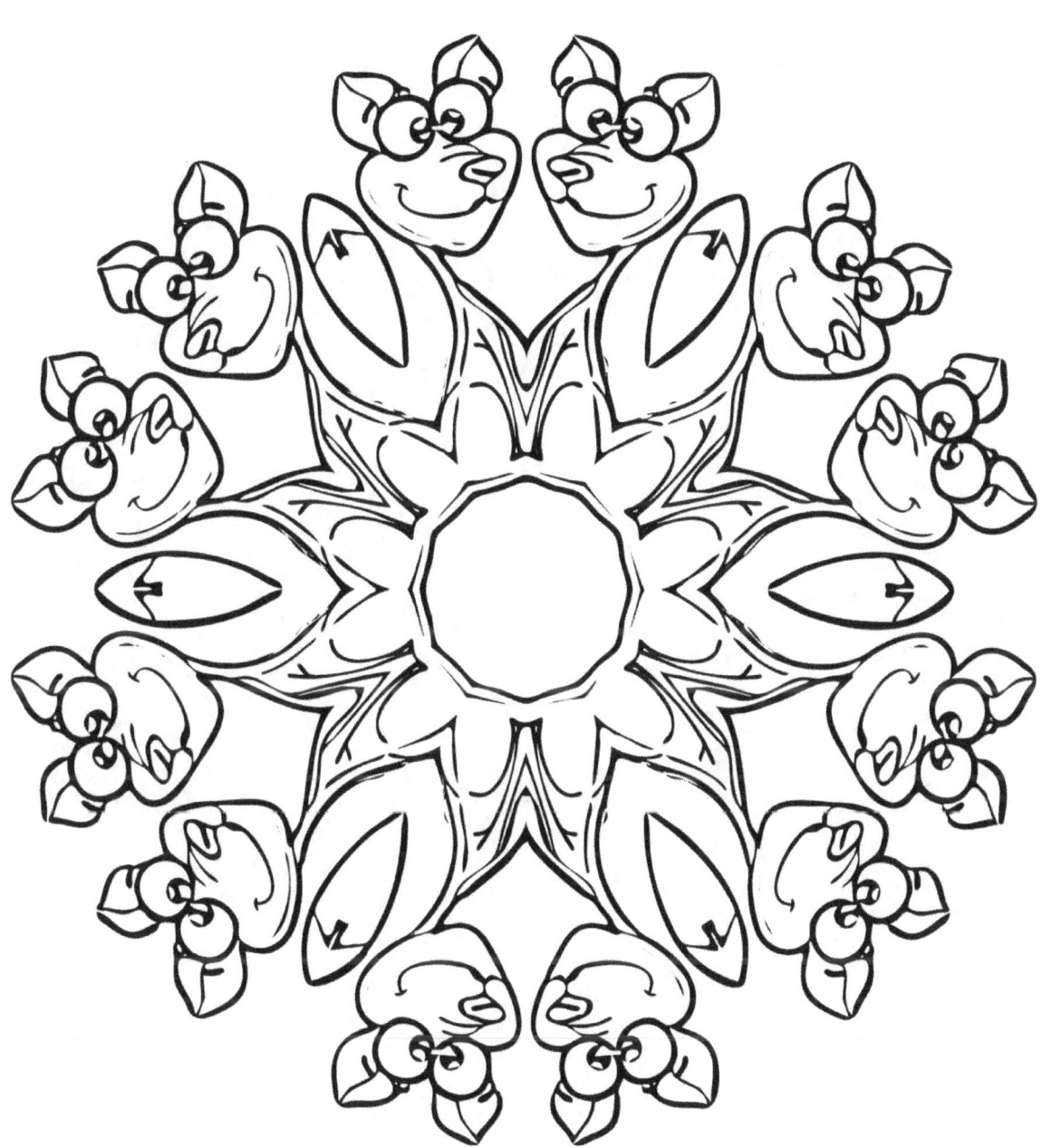

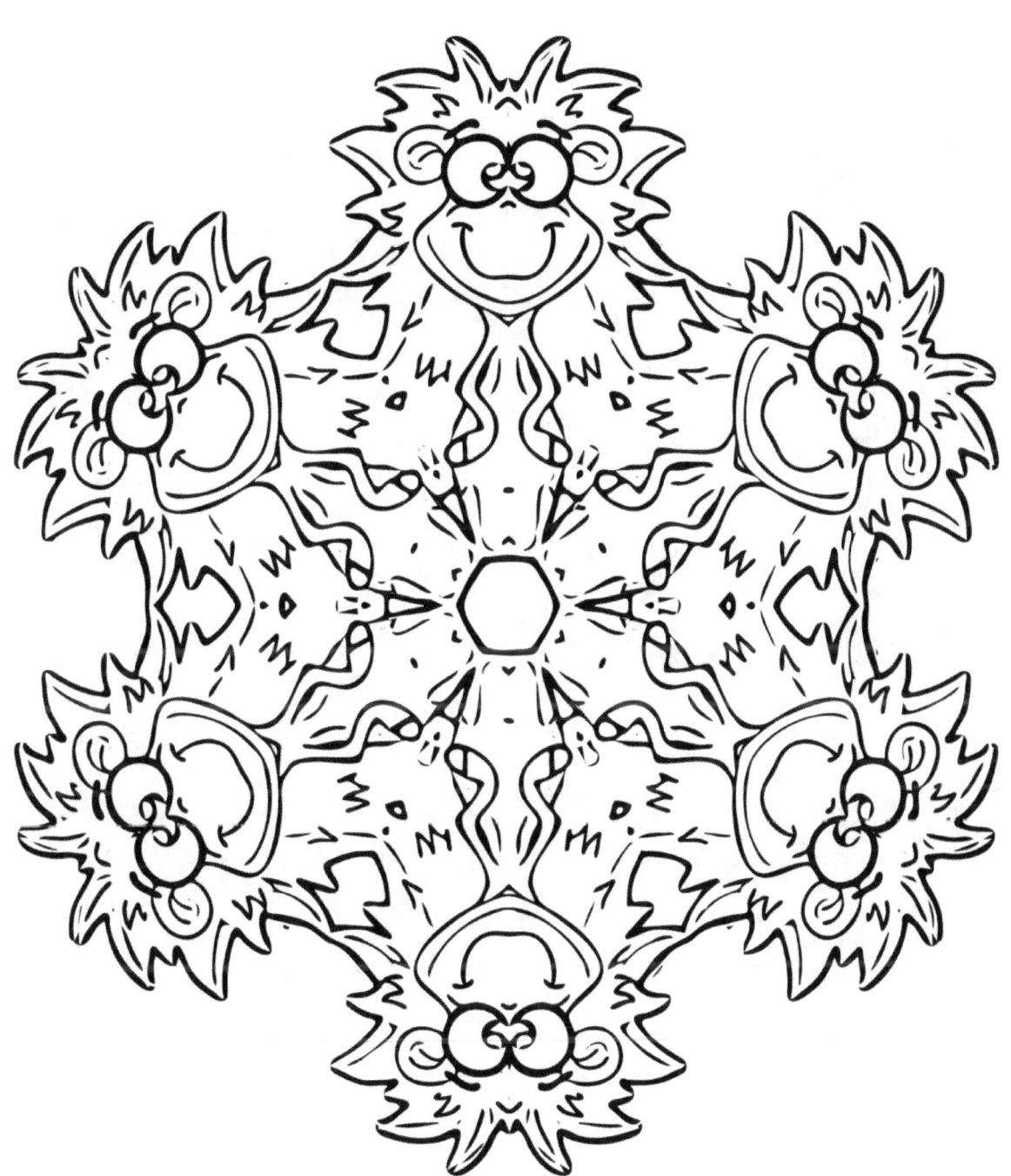

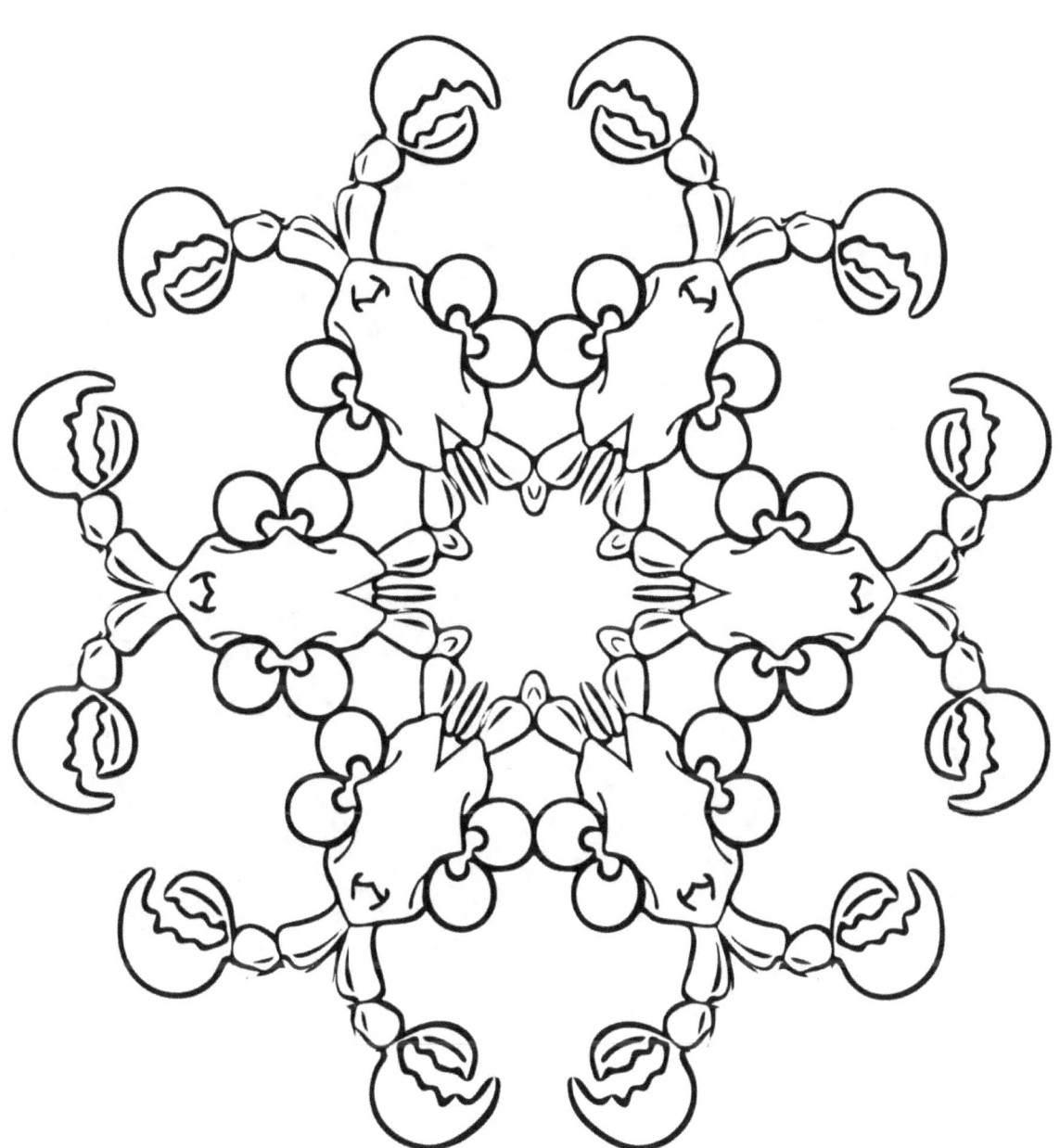

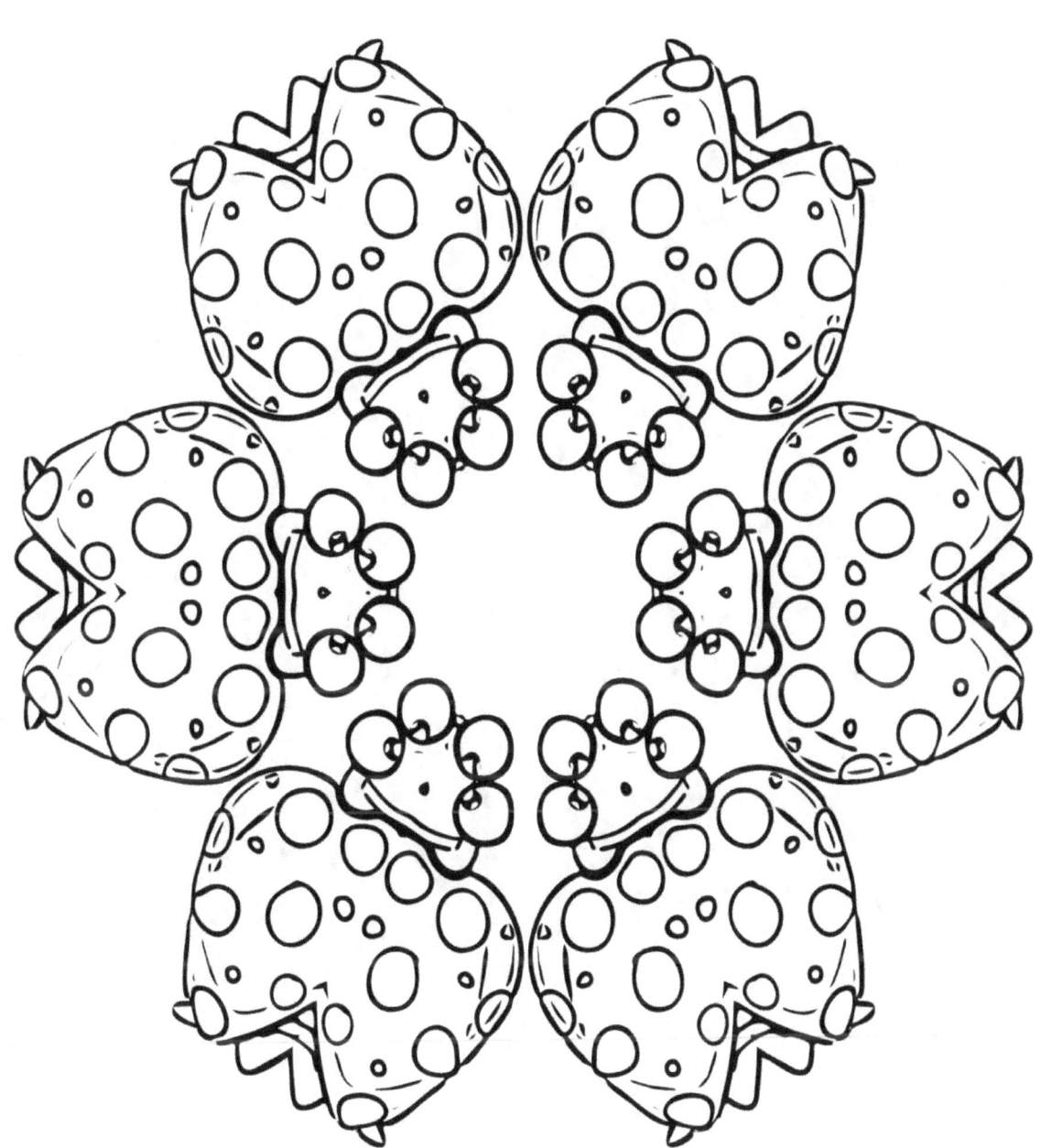

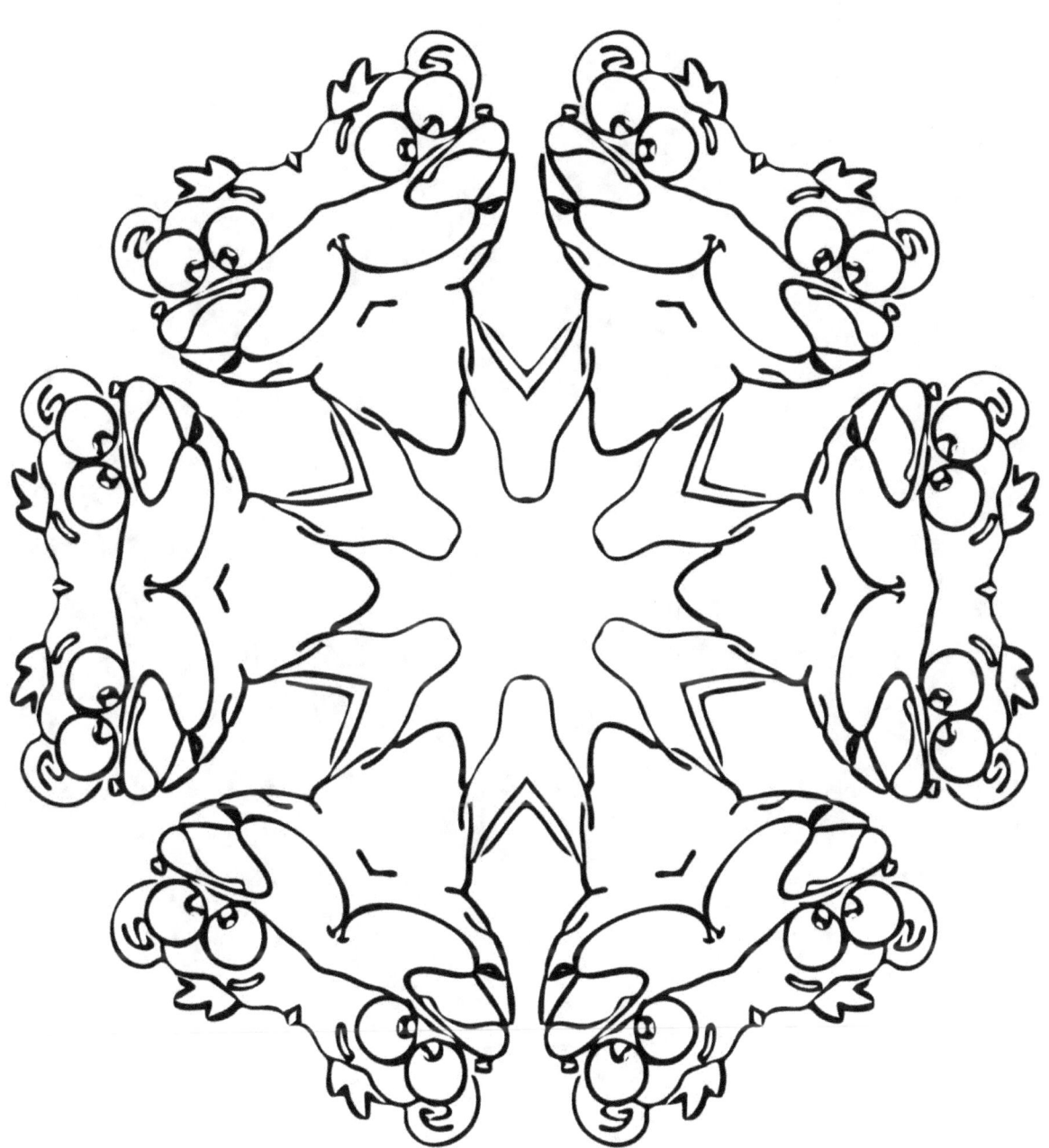

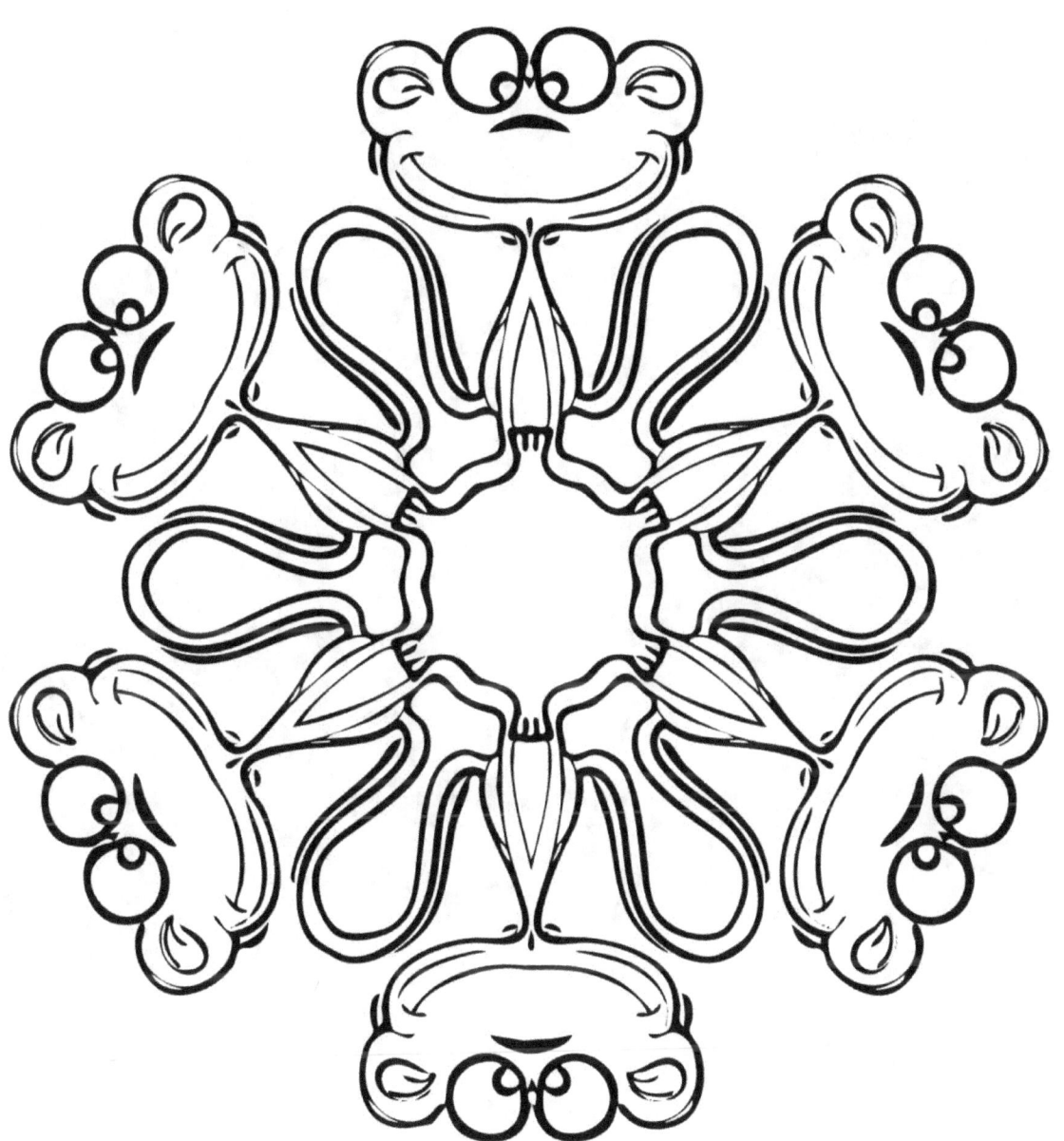

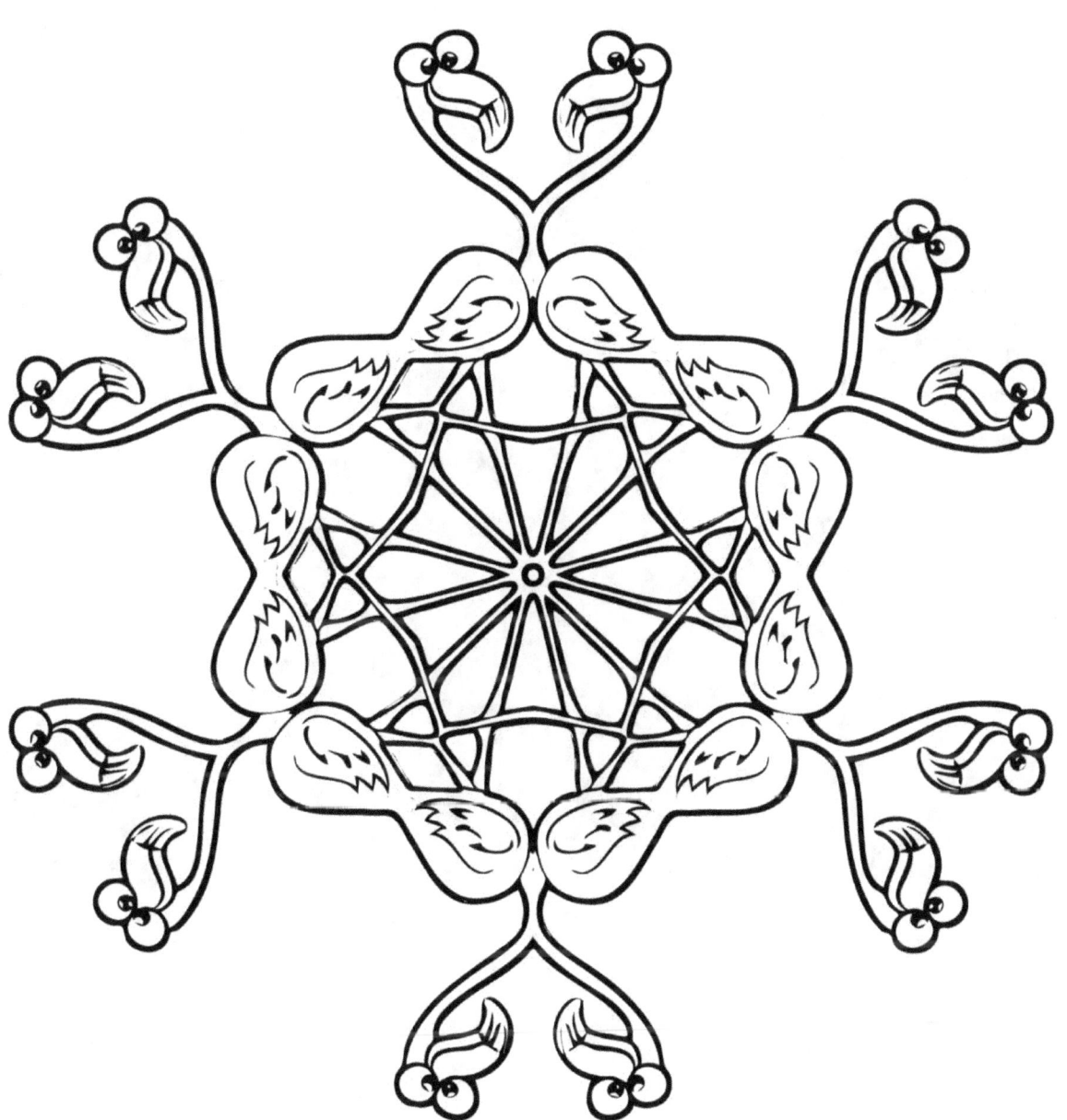

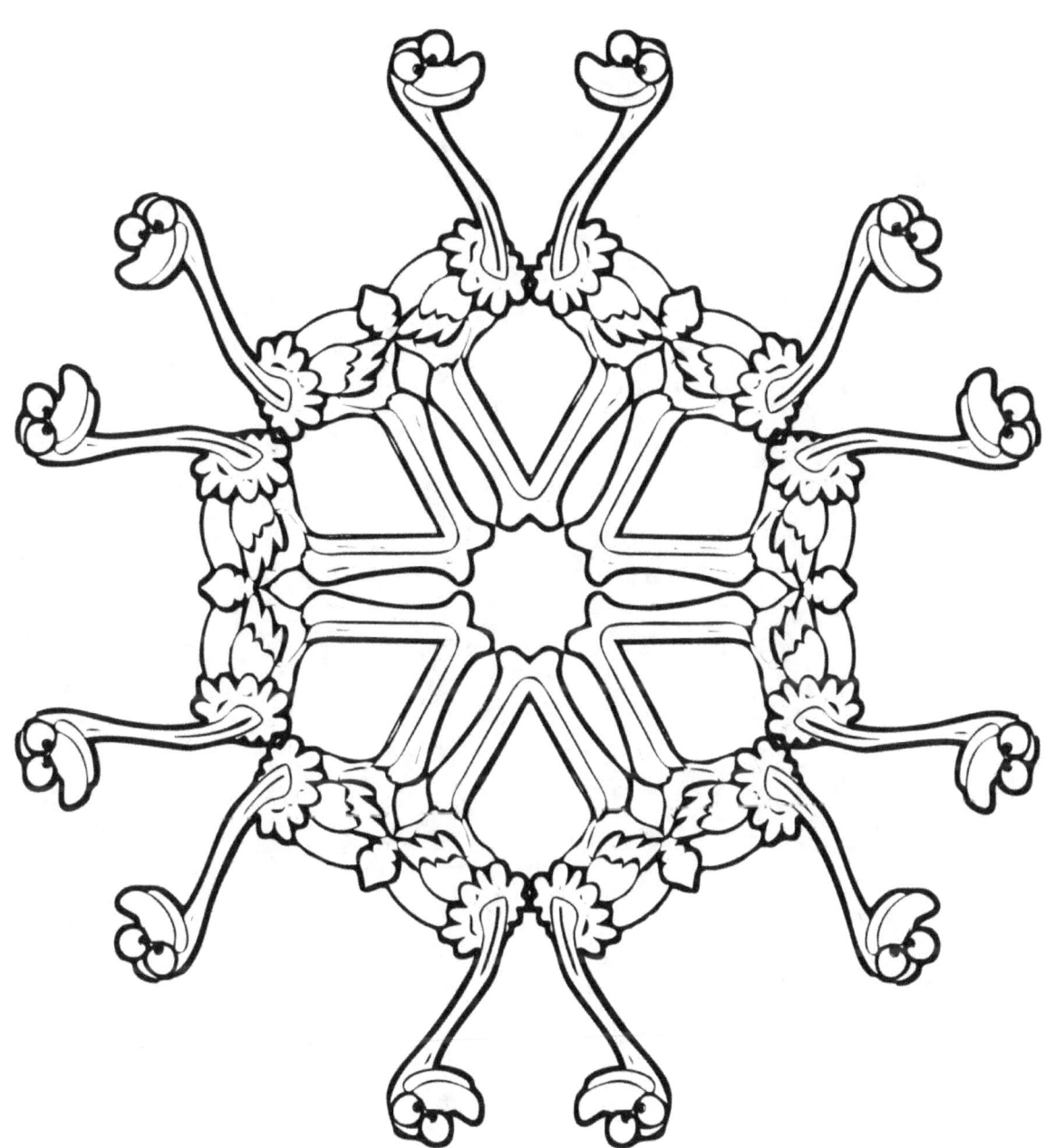

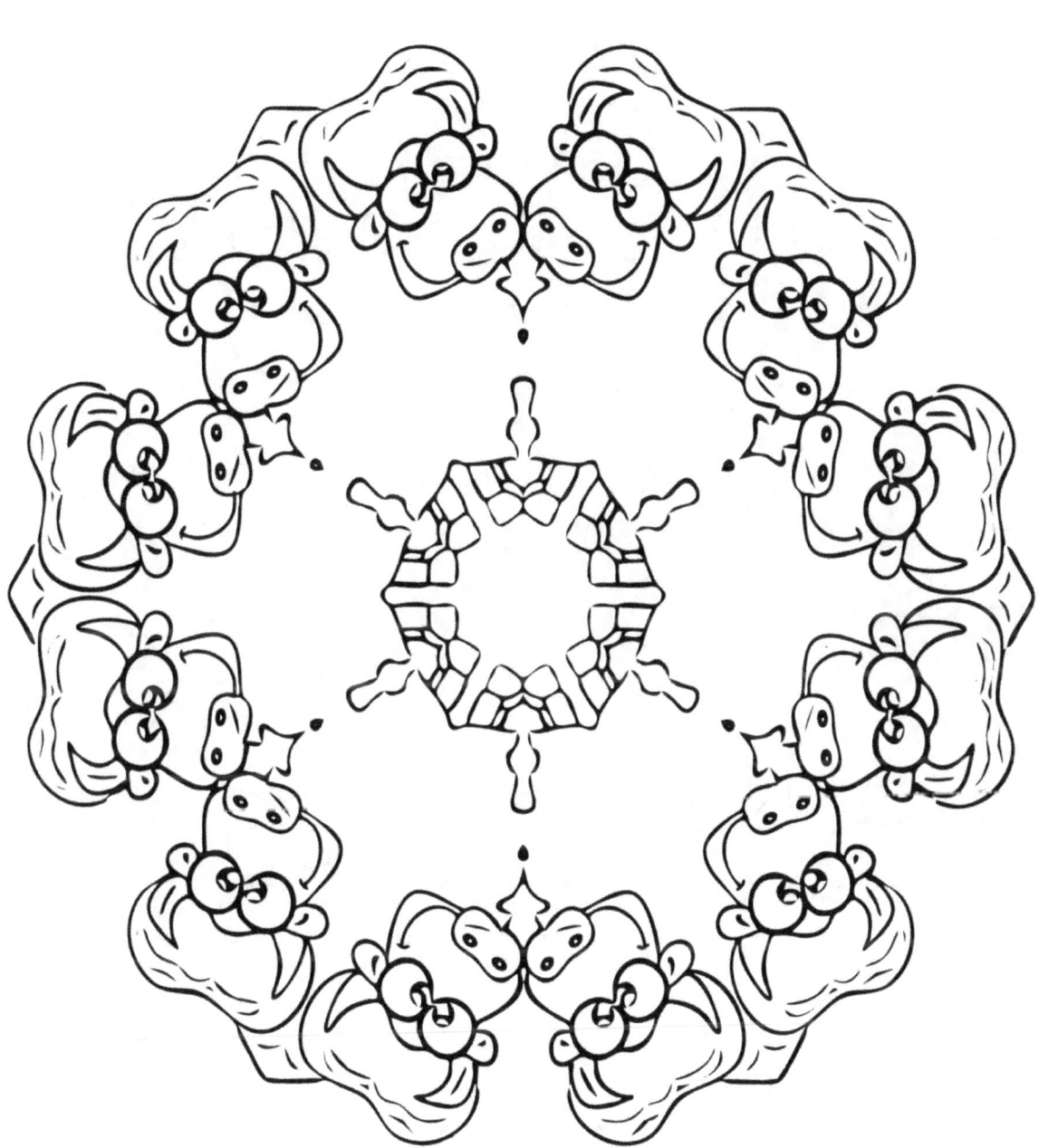

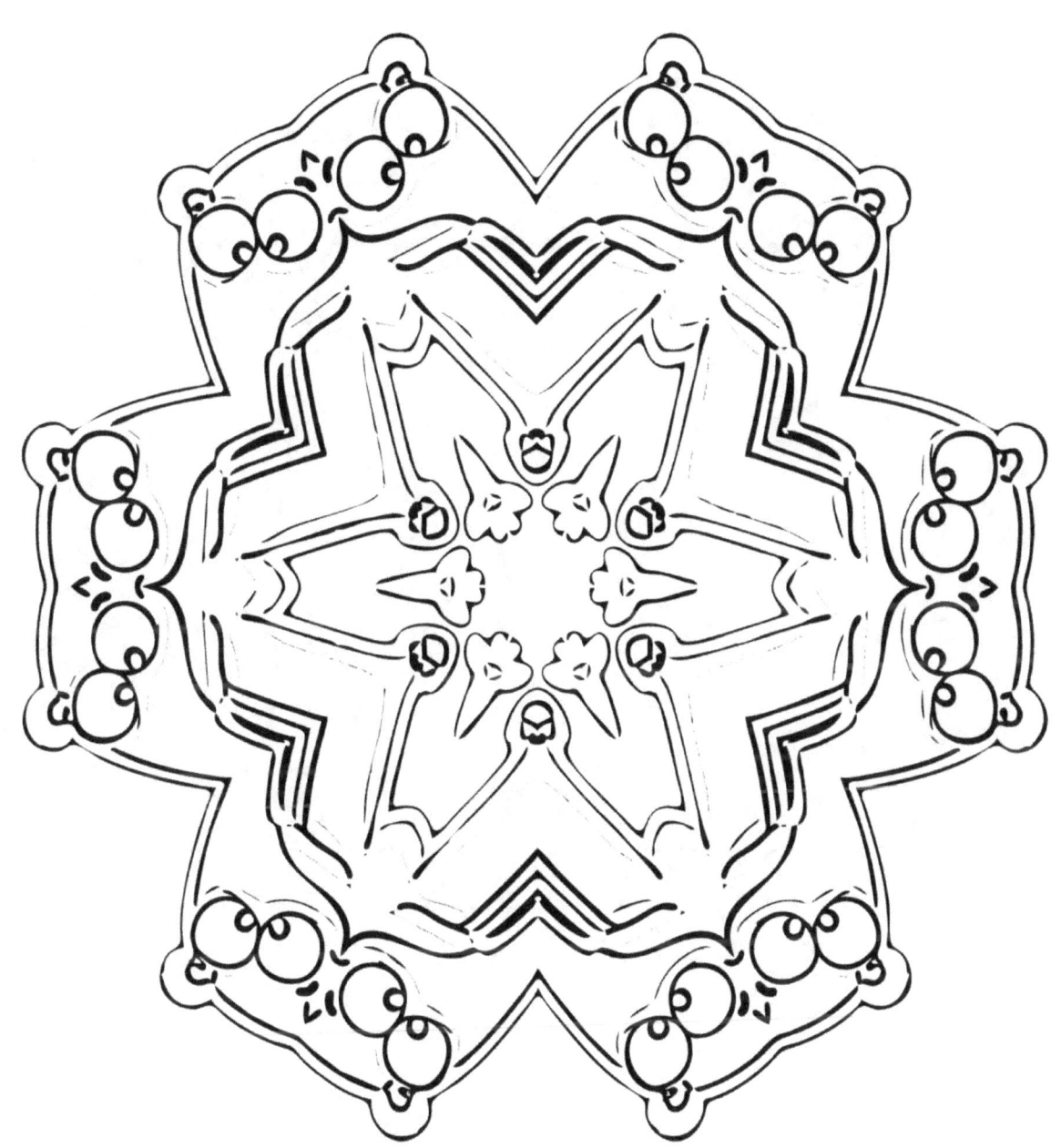

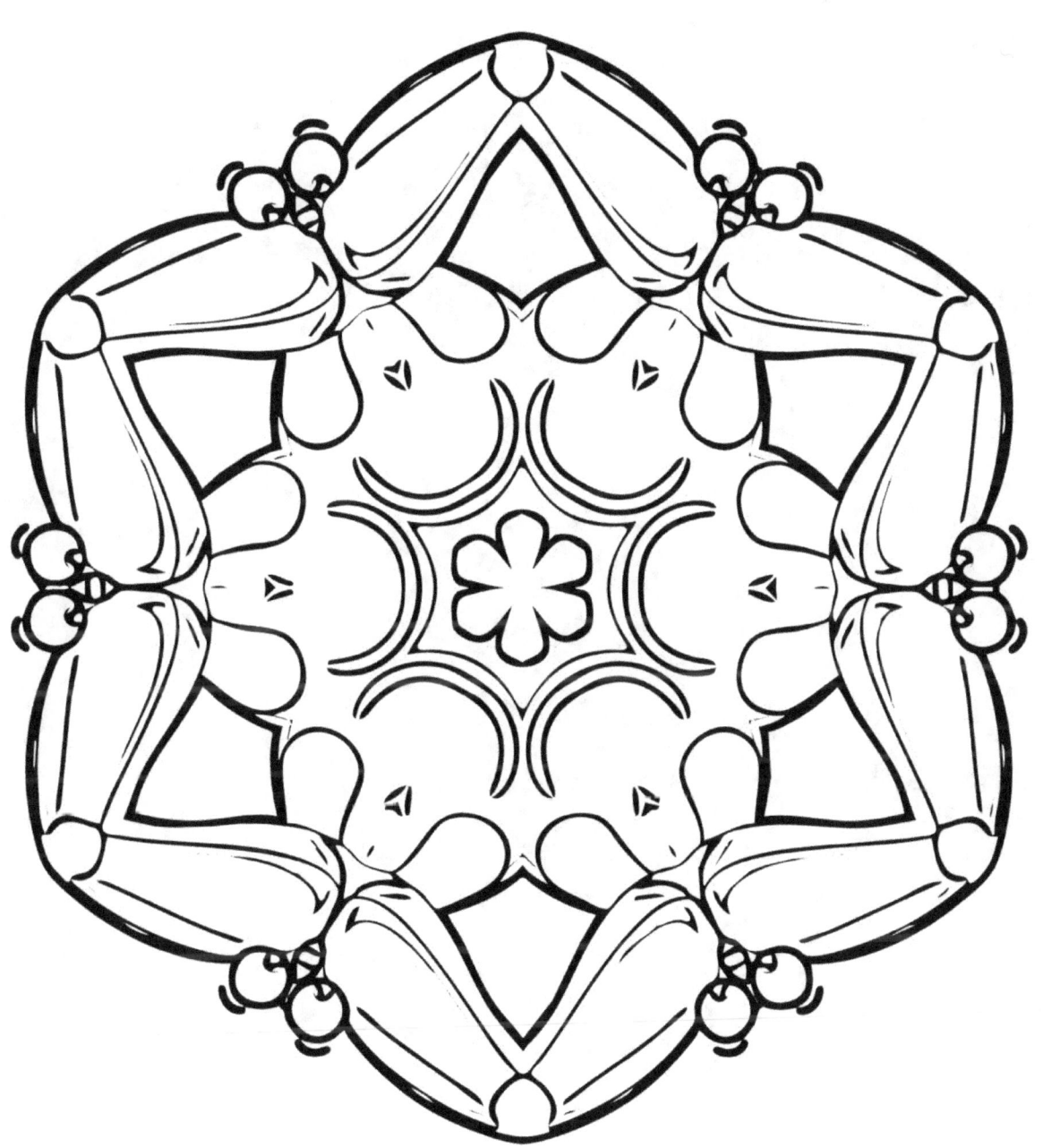

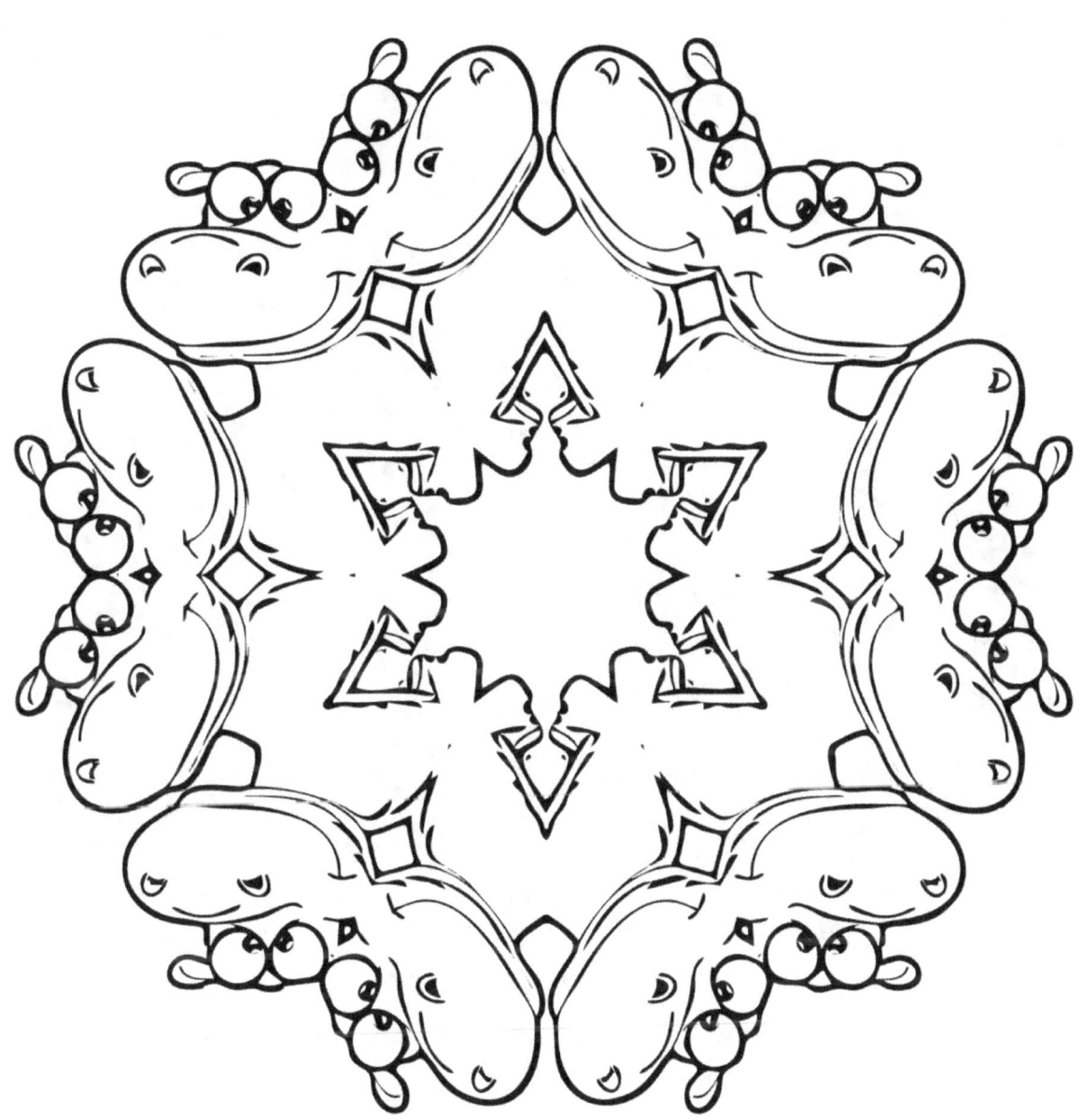

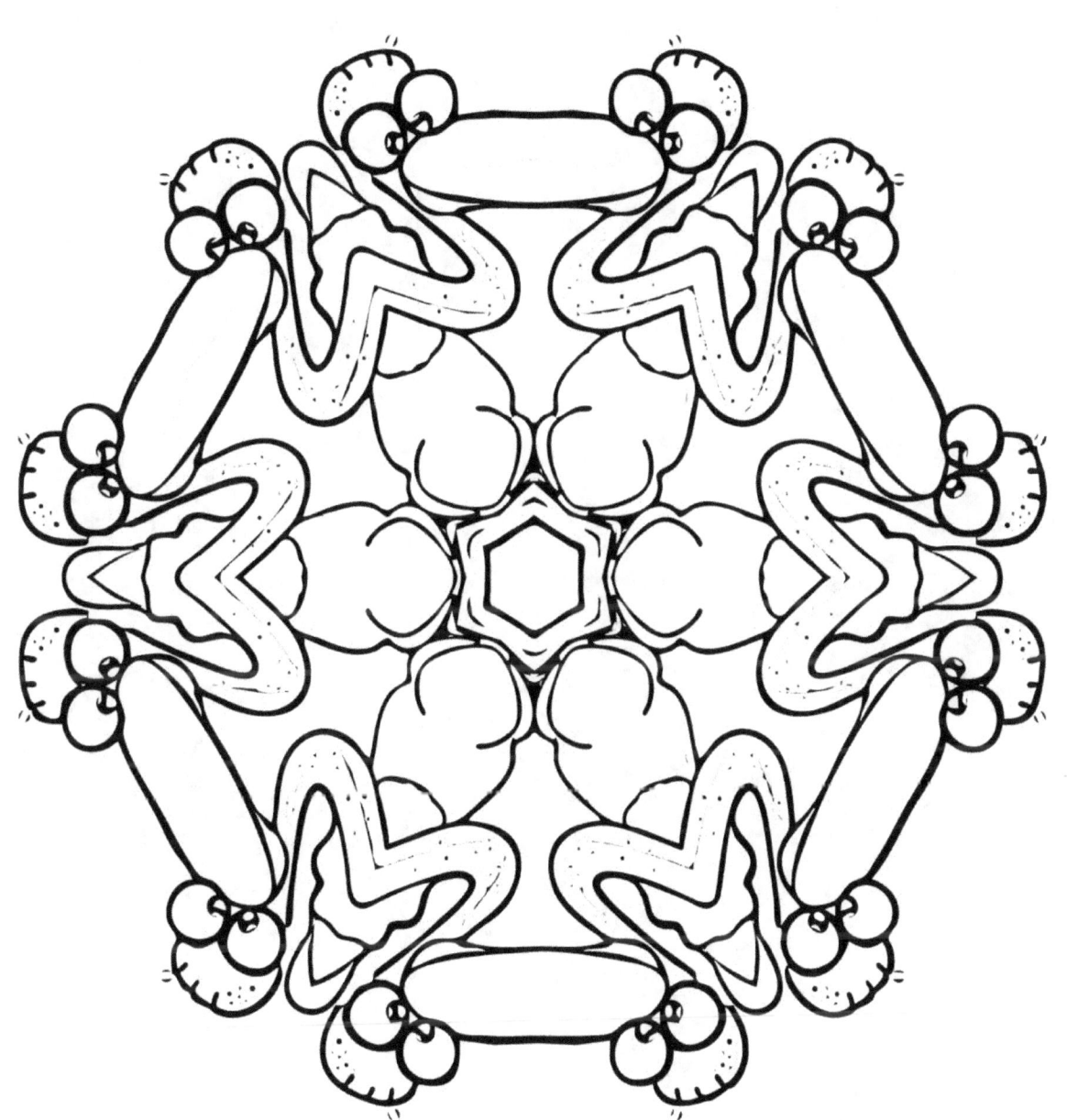

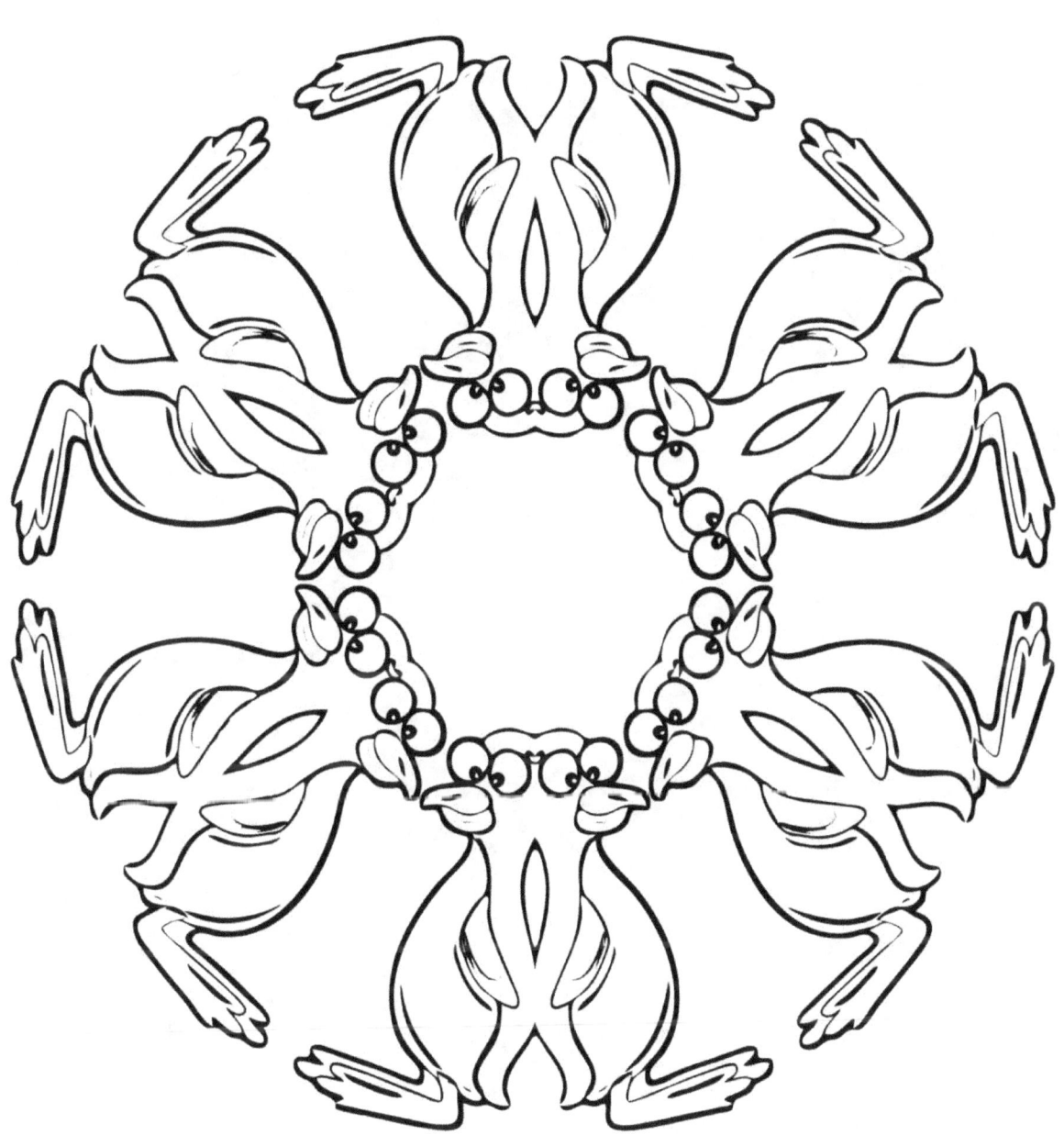

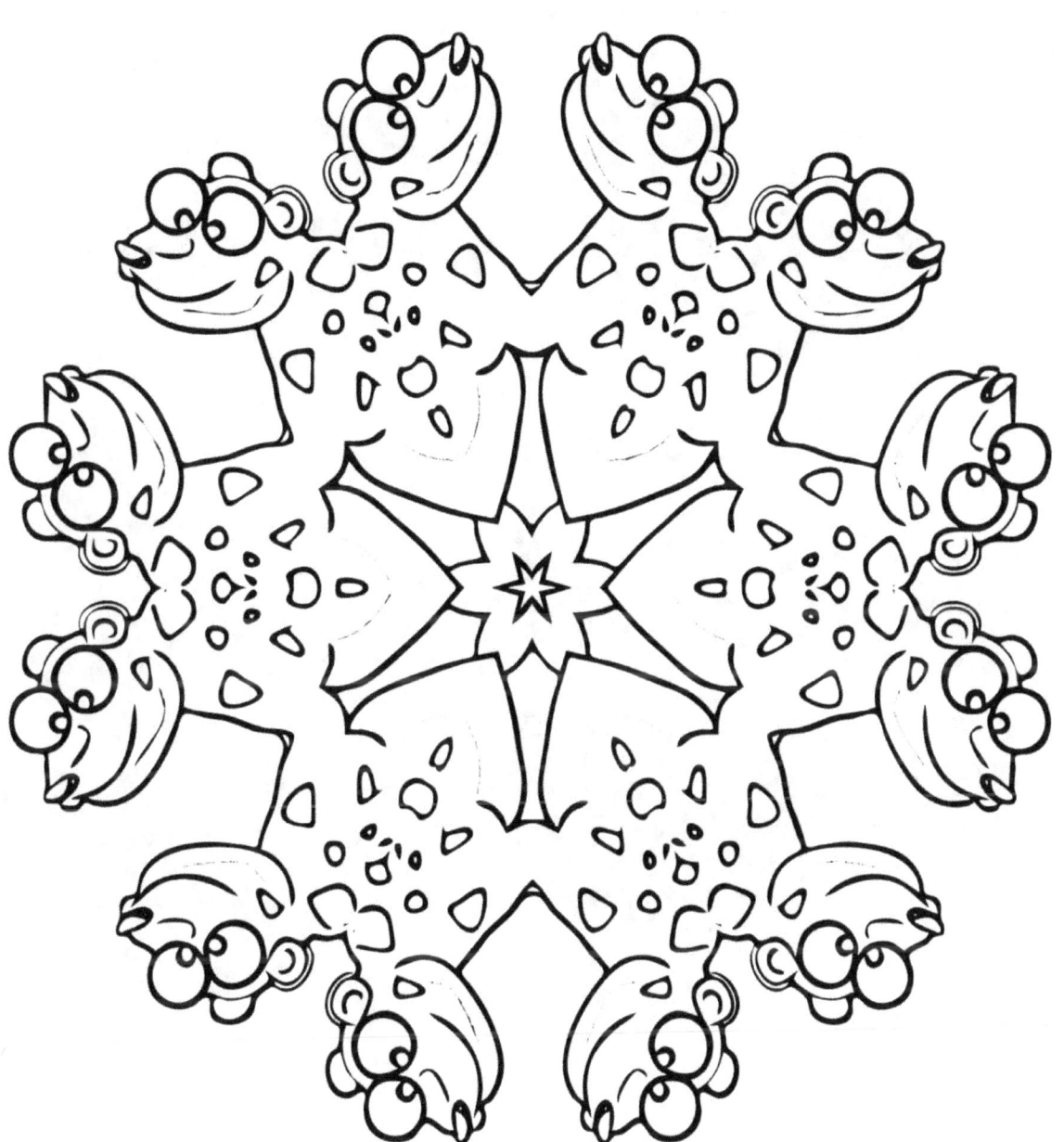

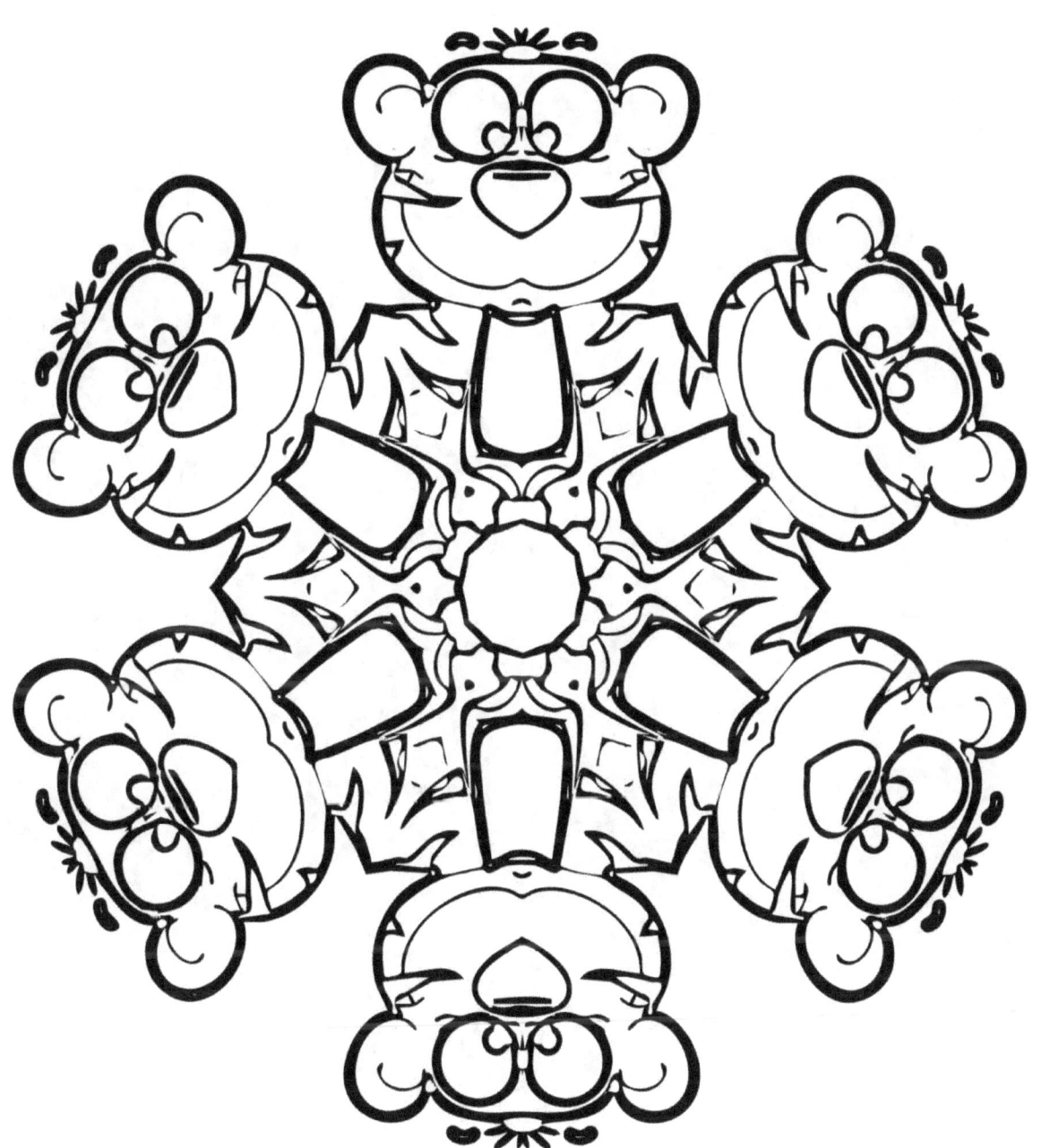

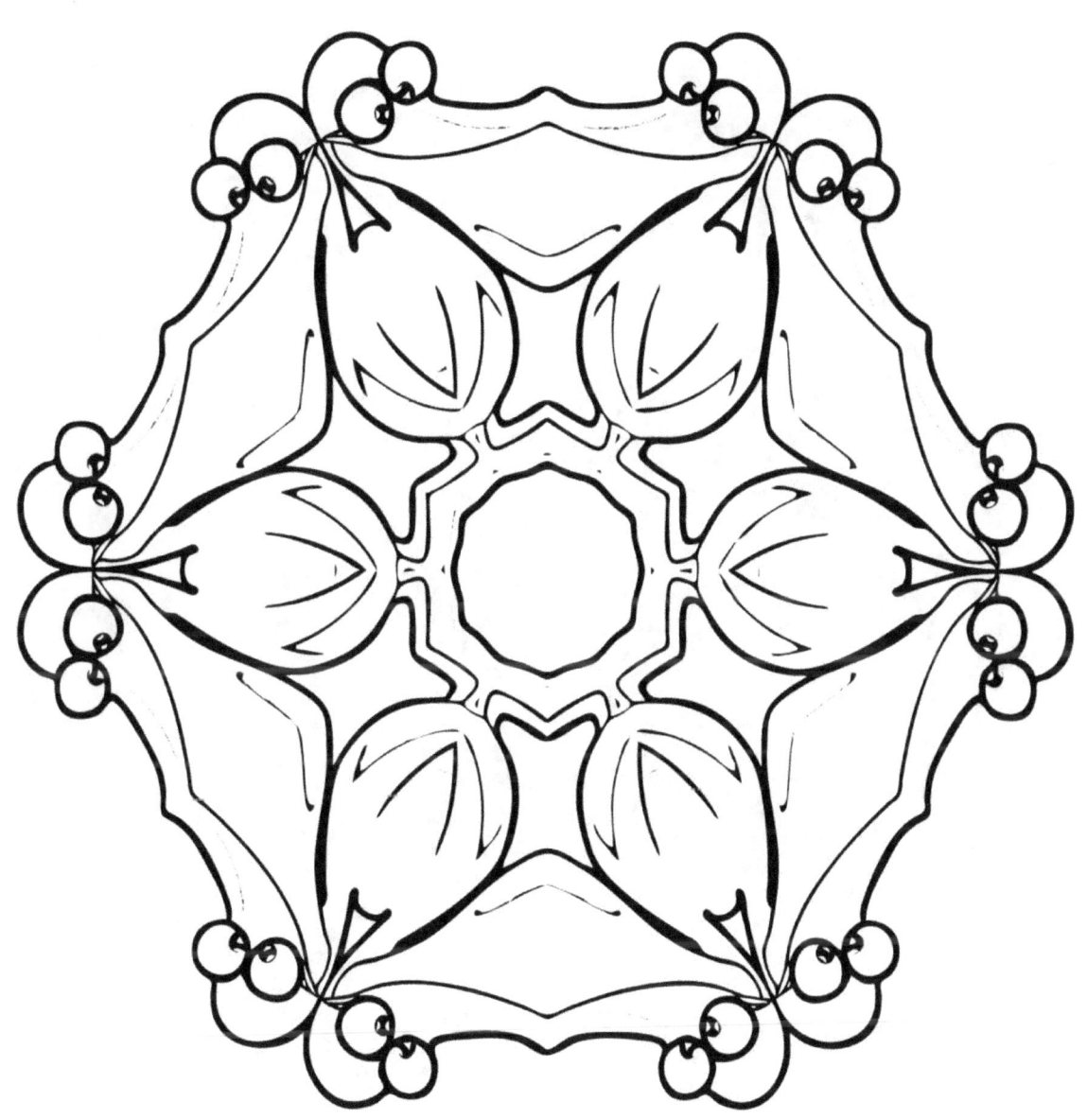

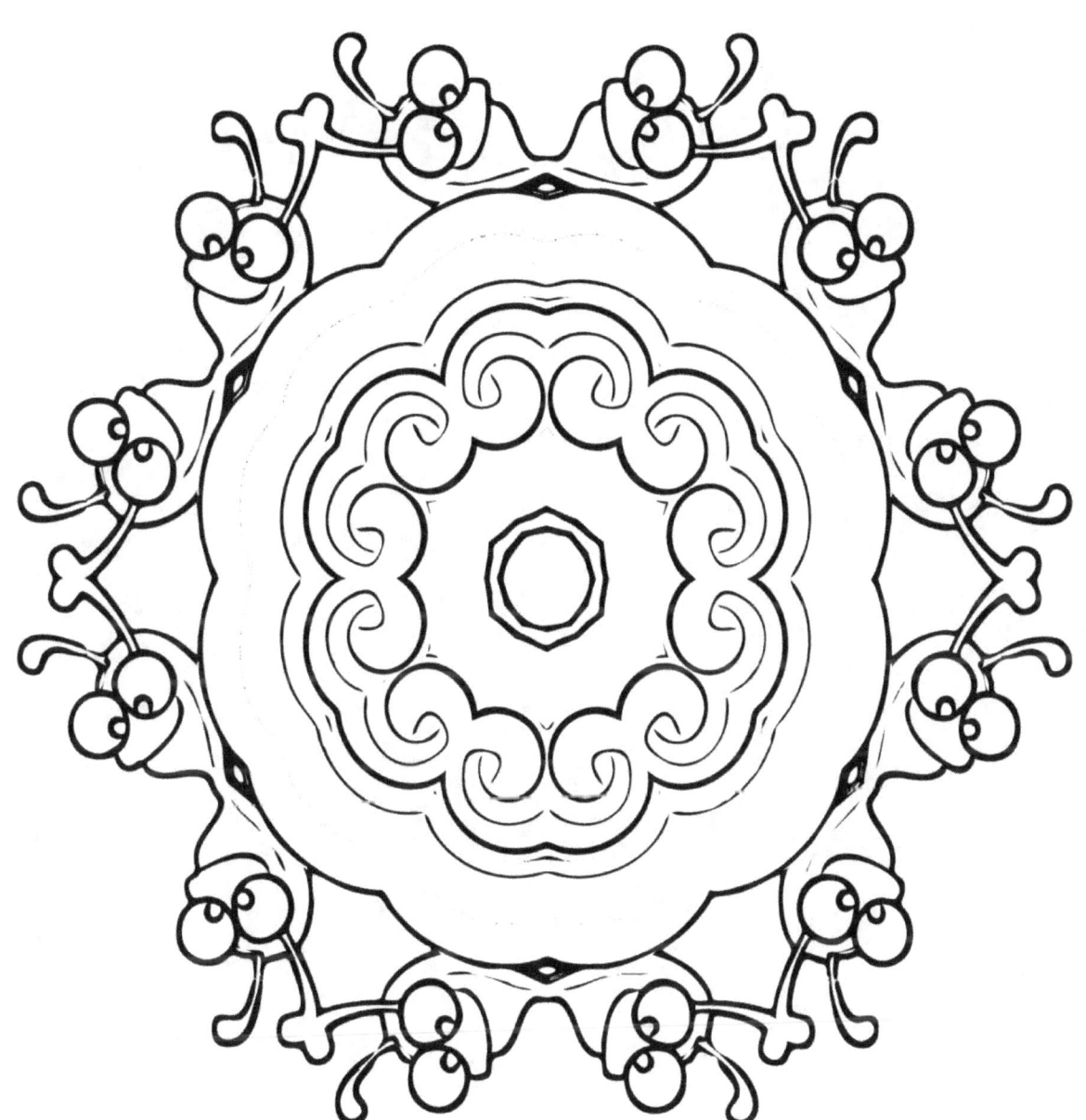

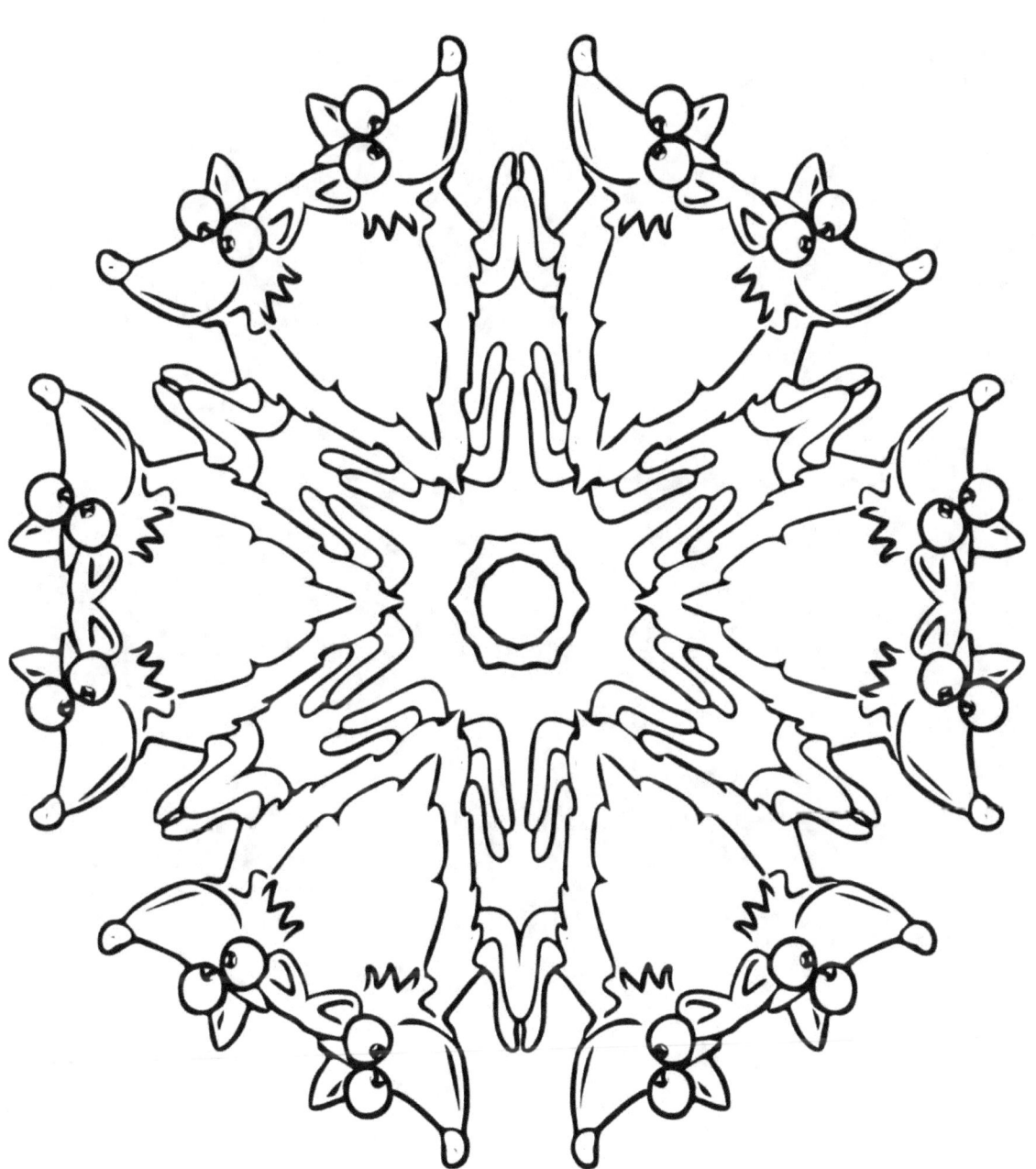

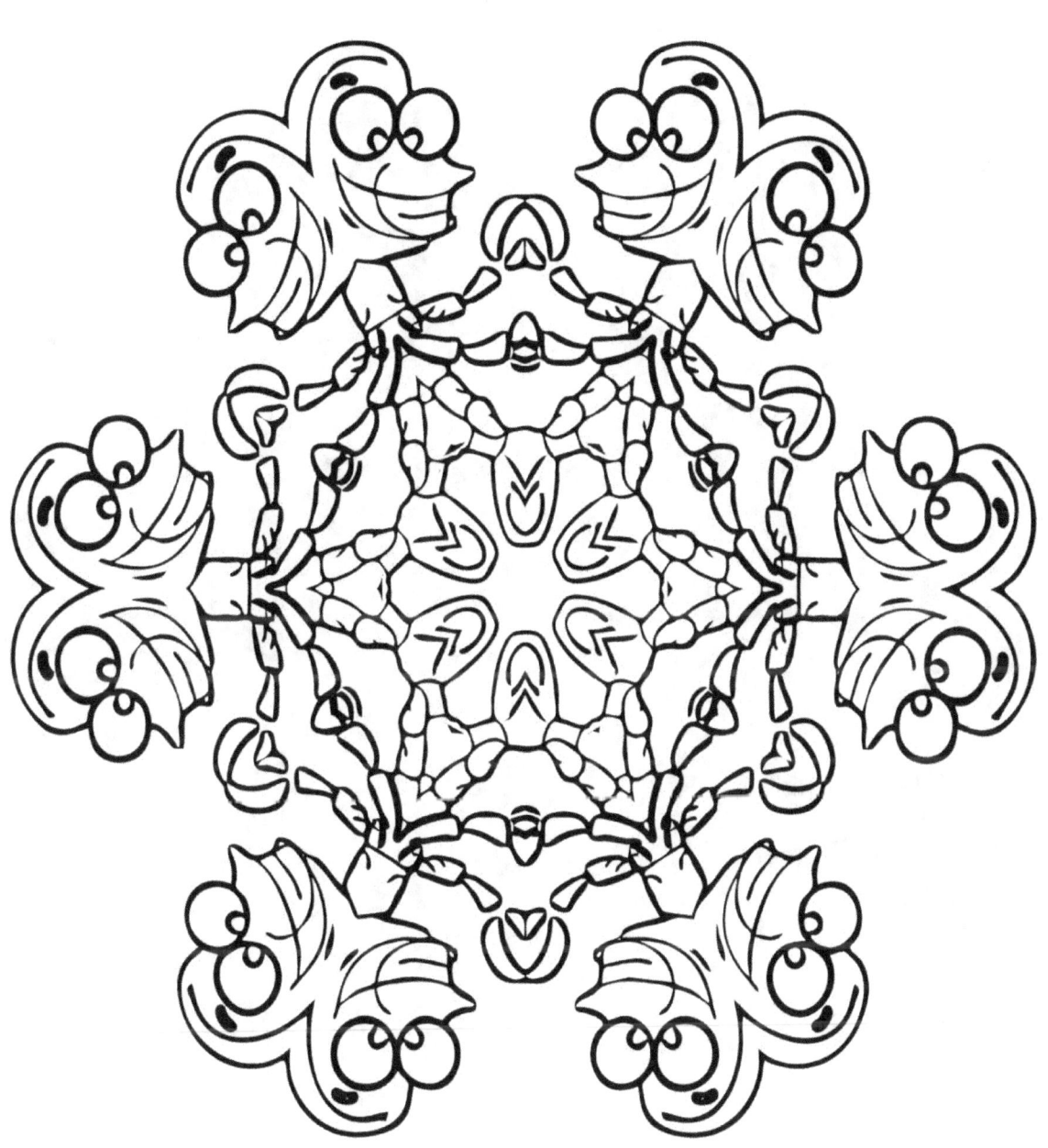

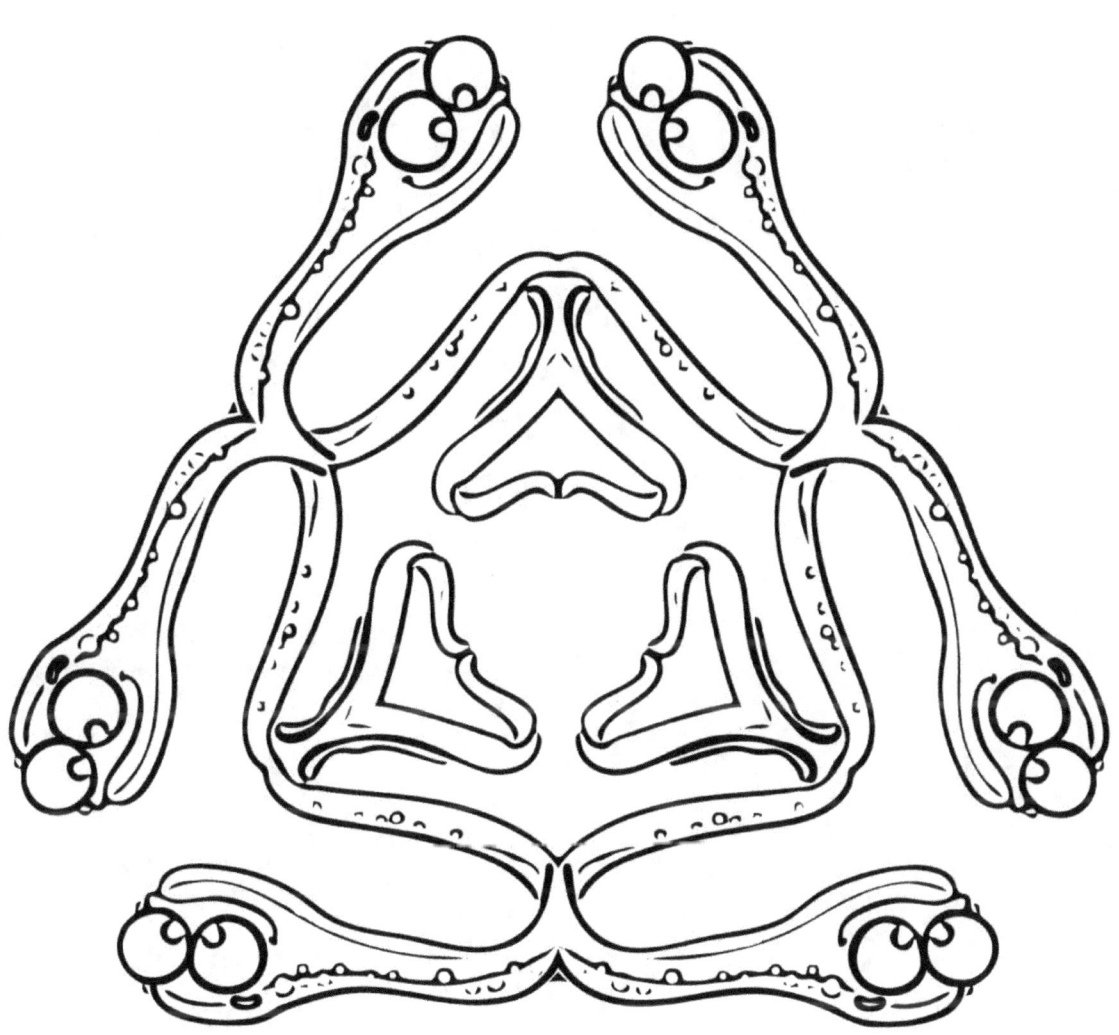

Ocean Coloring Book

PSYCHEDELIC STRESS-RELIEVING FISH

A Coloring Book For Adults

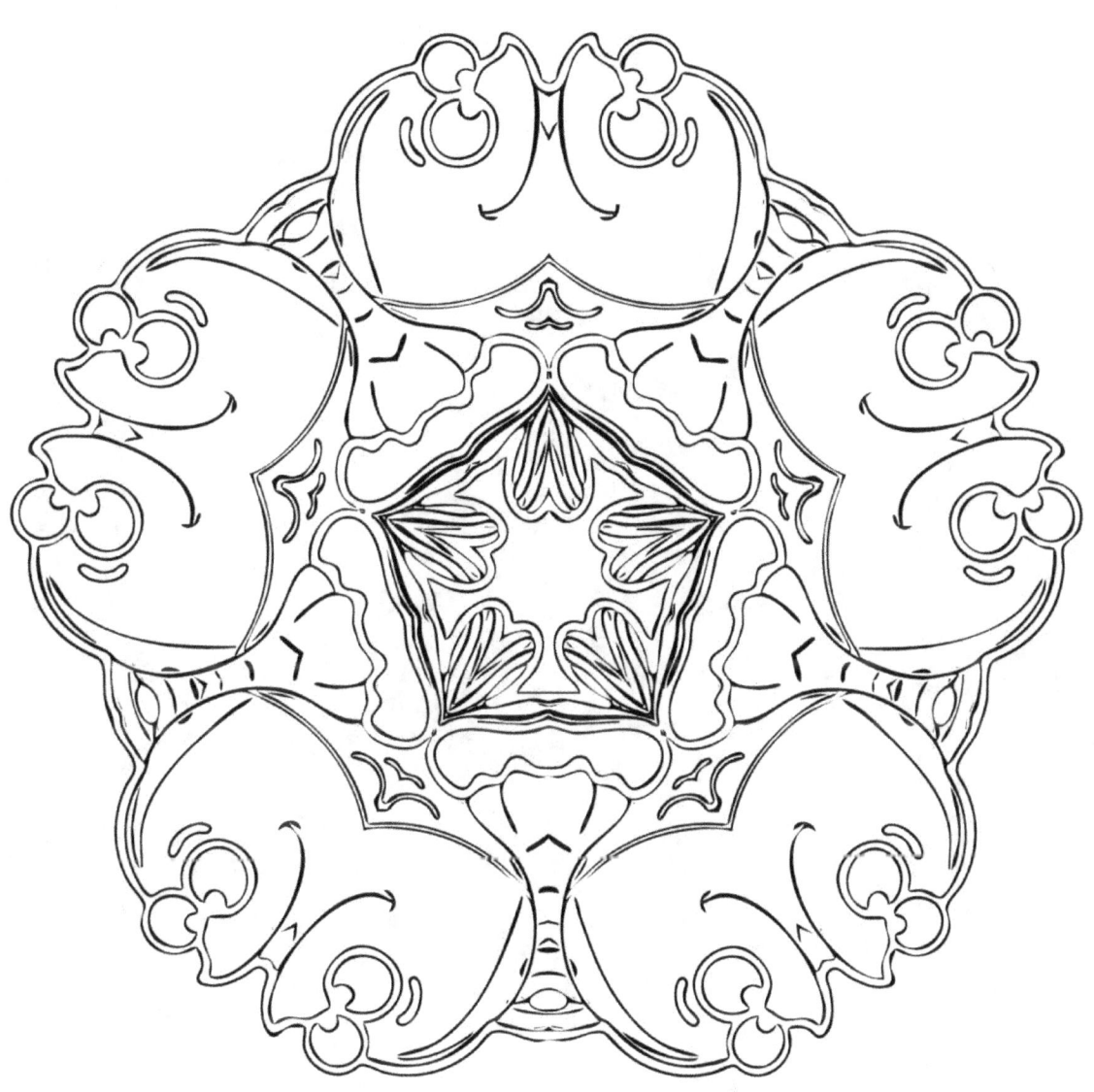

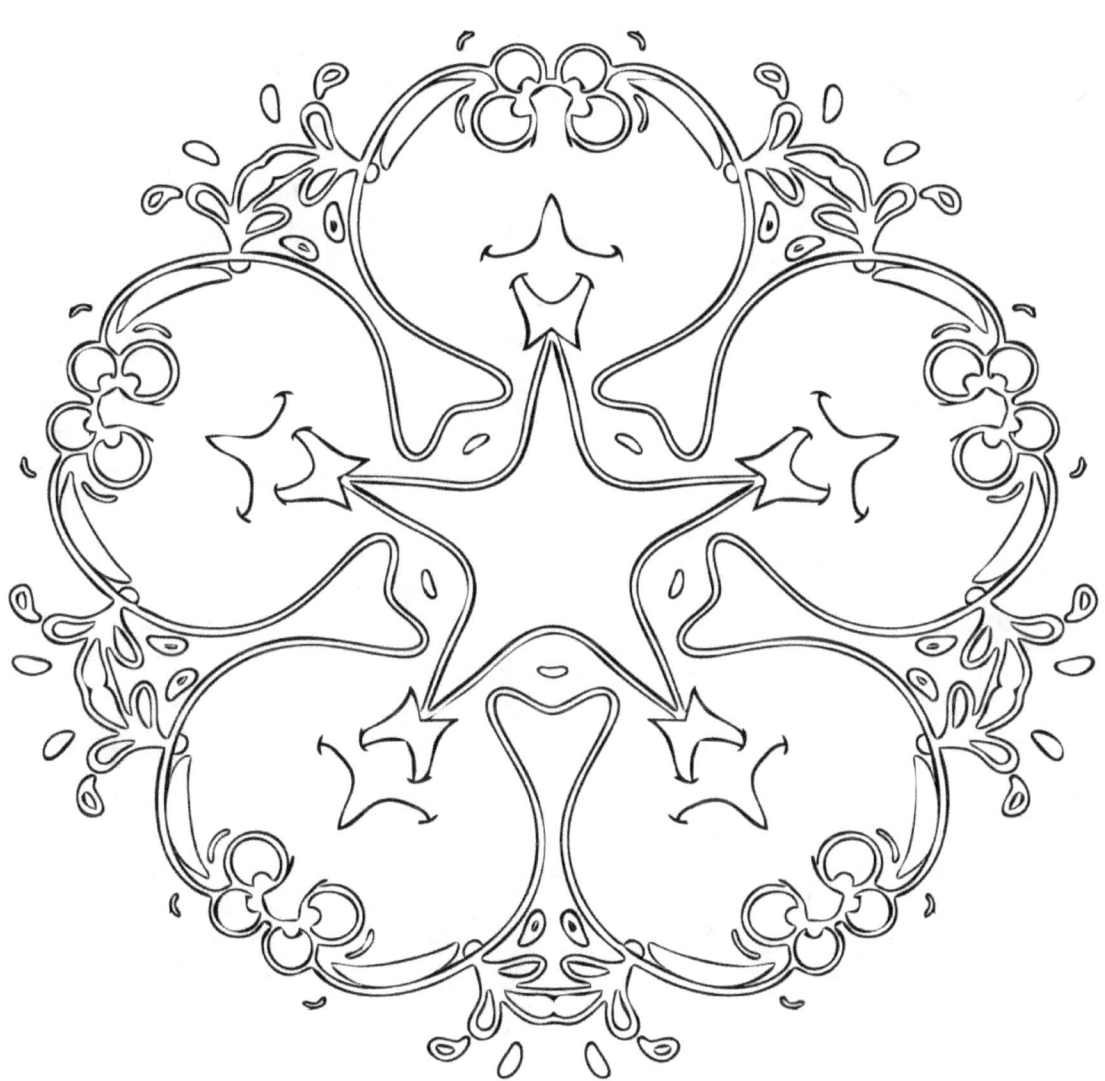

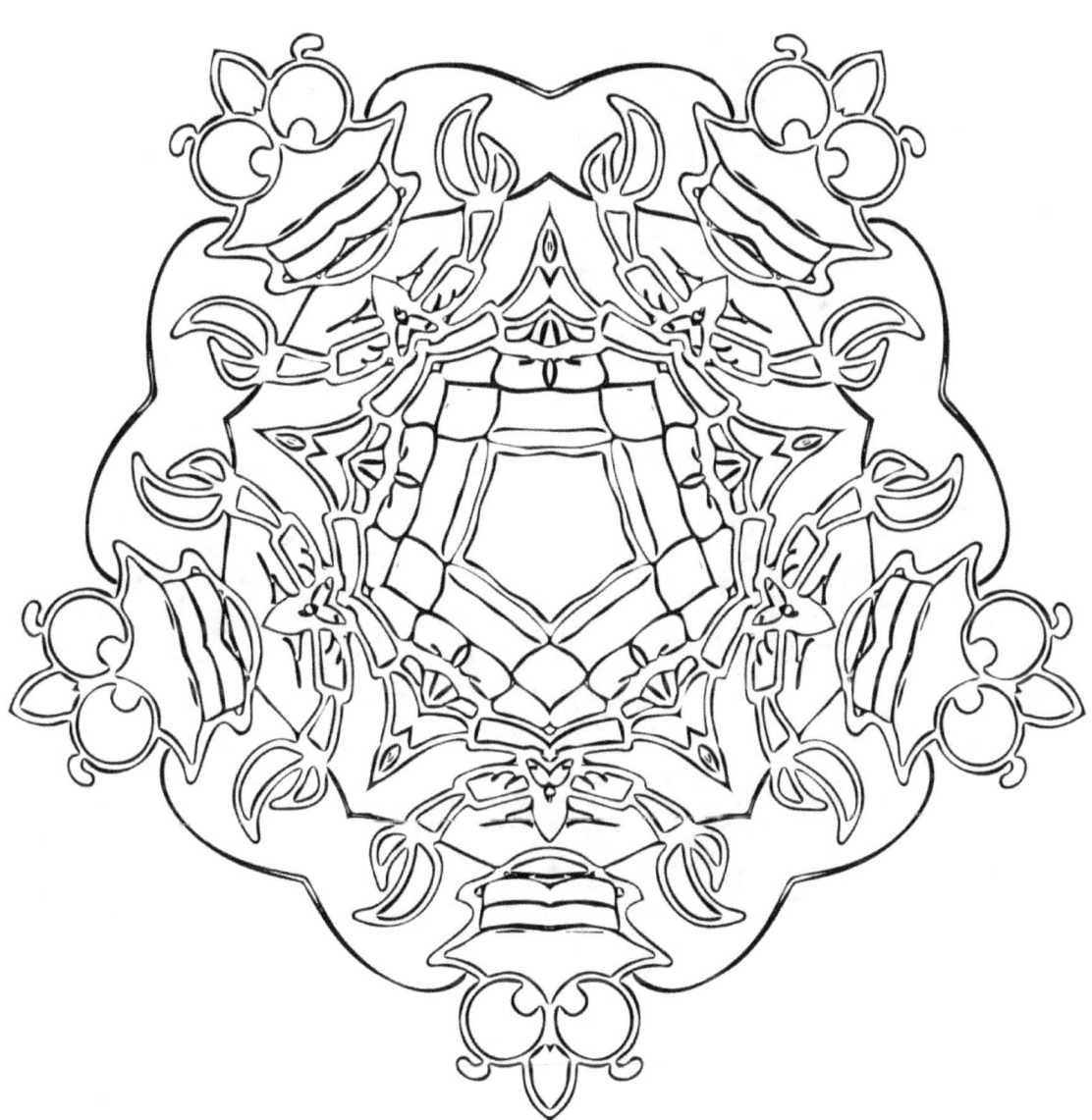

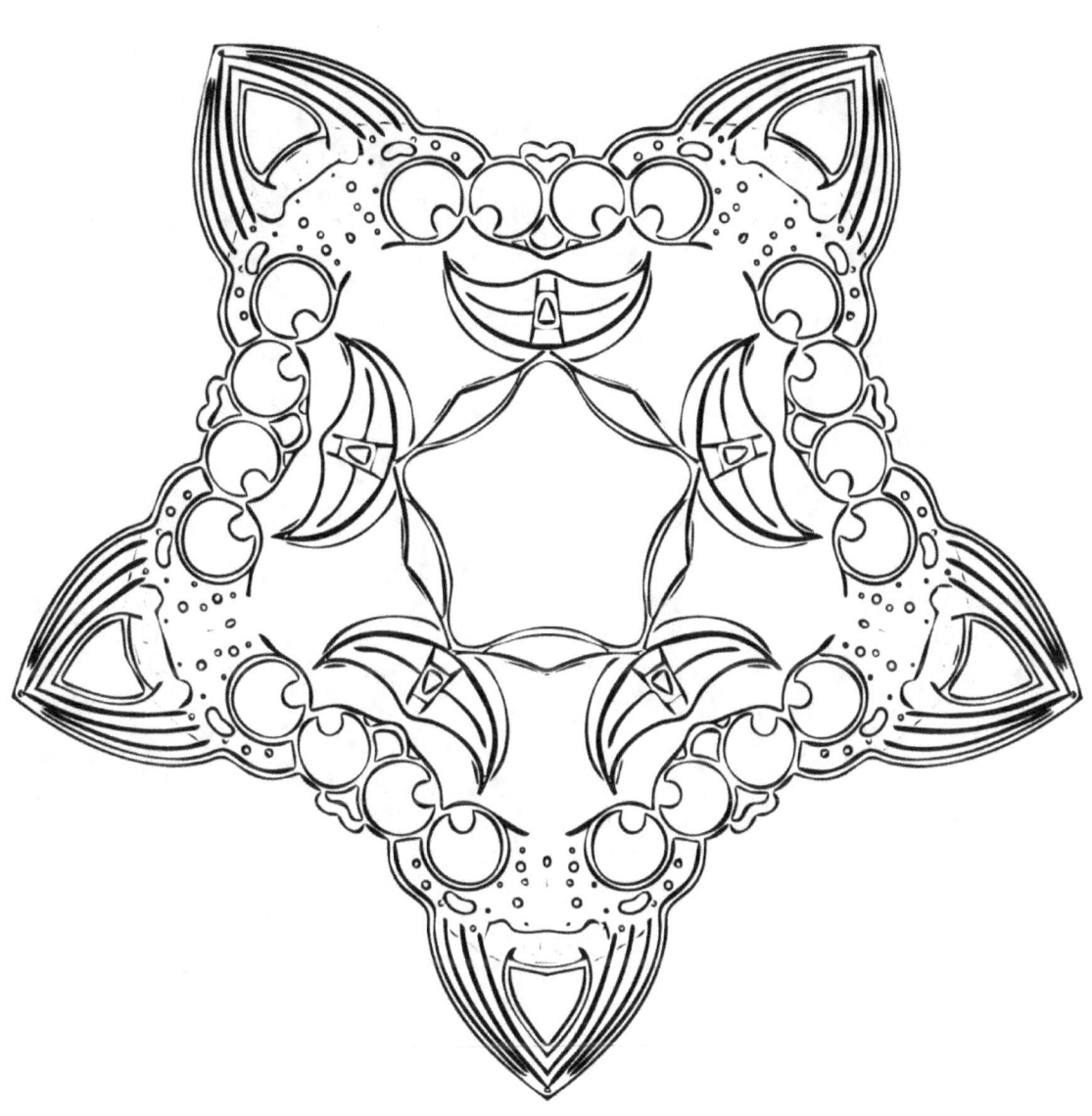

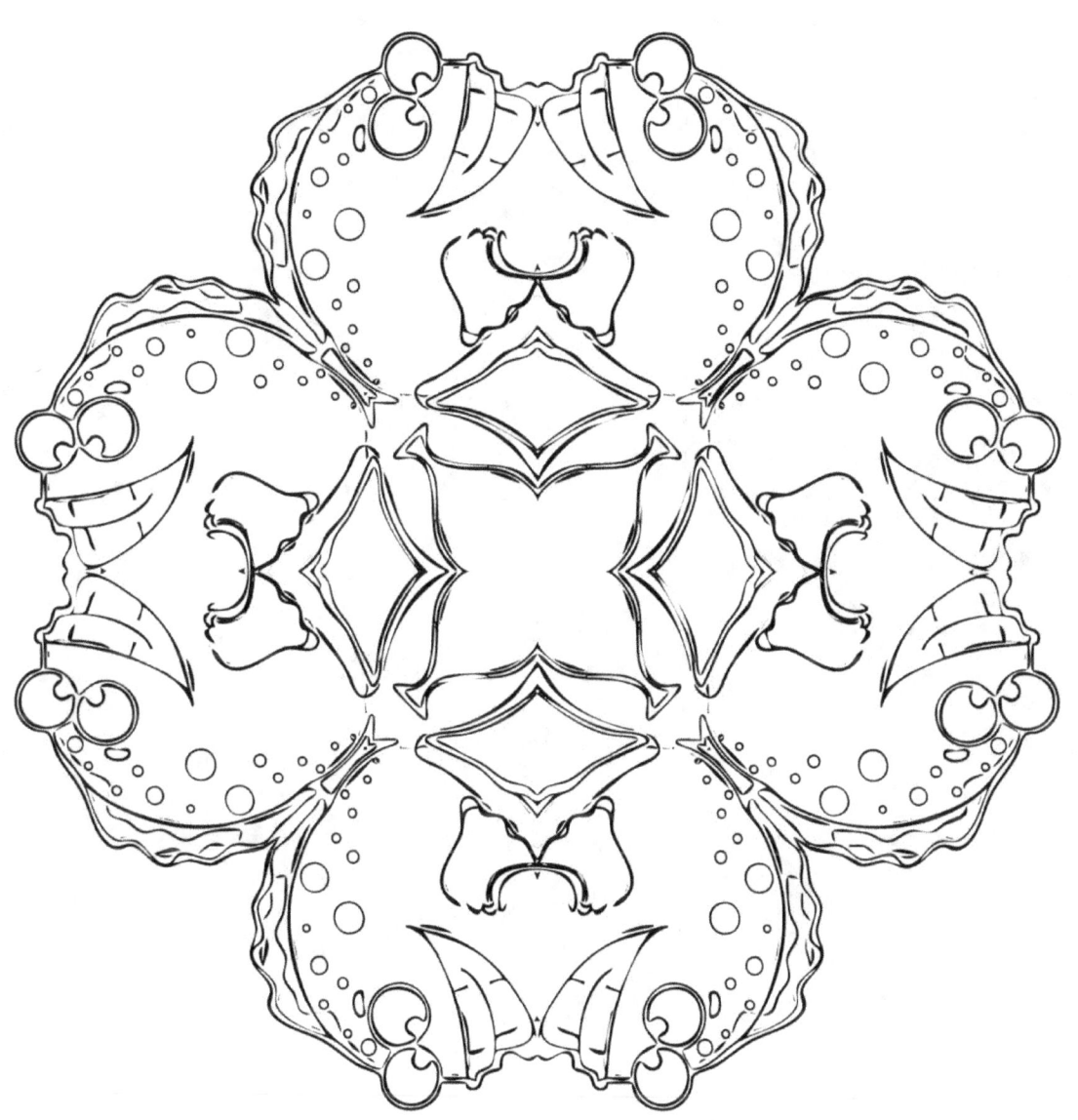

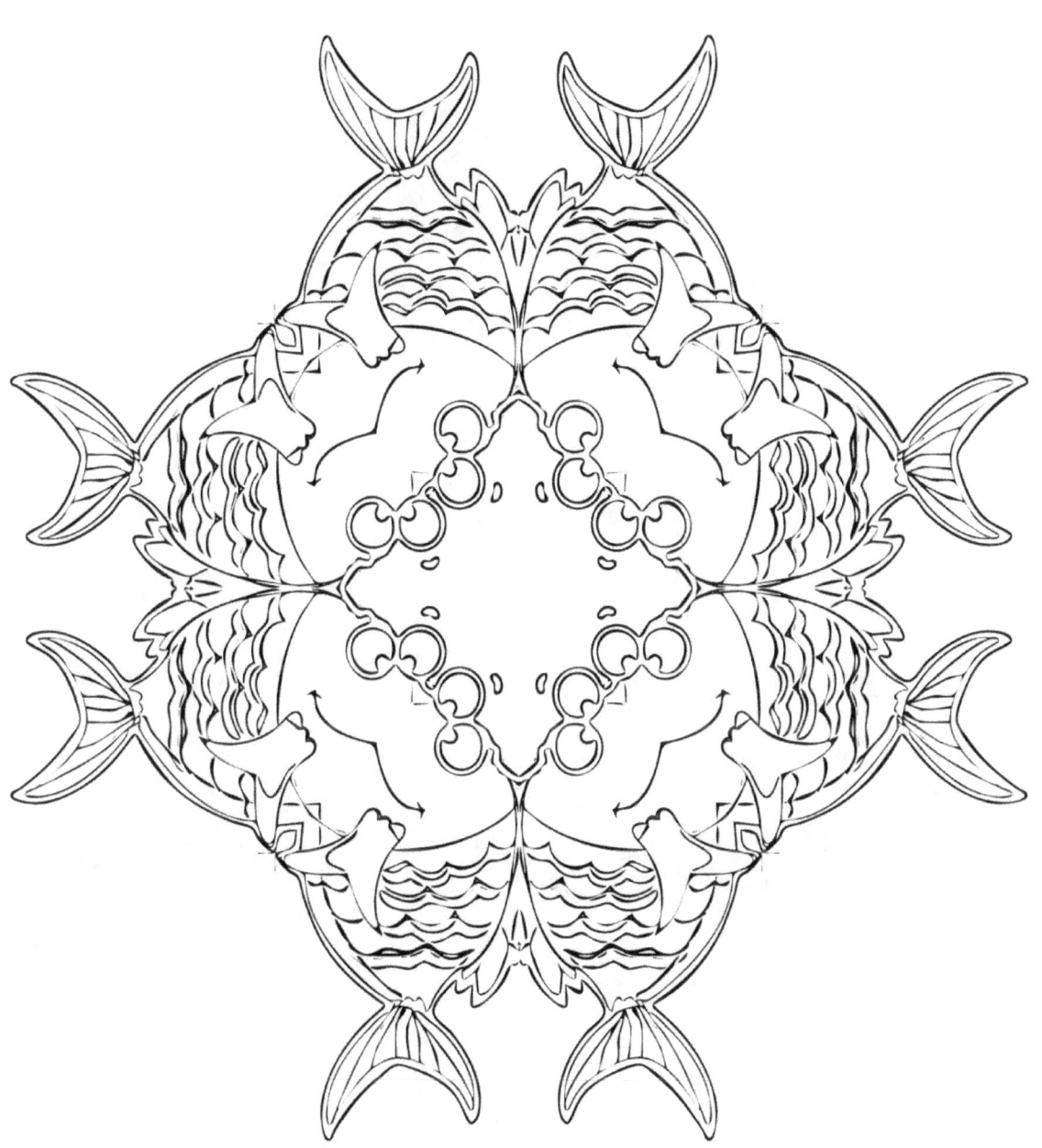

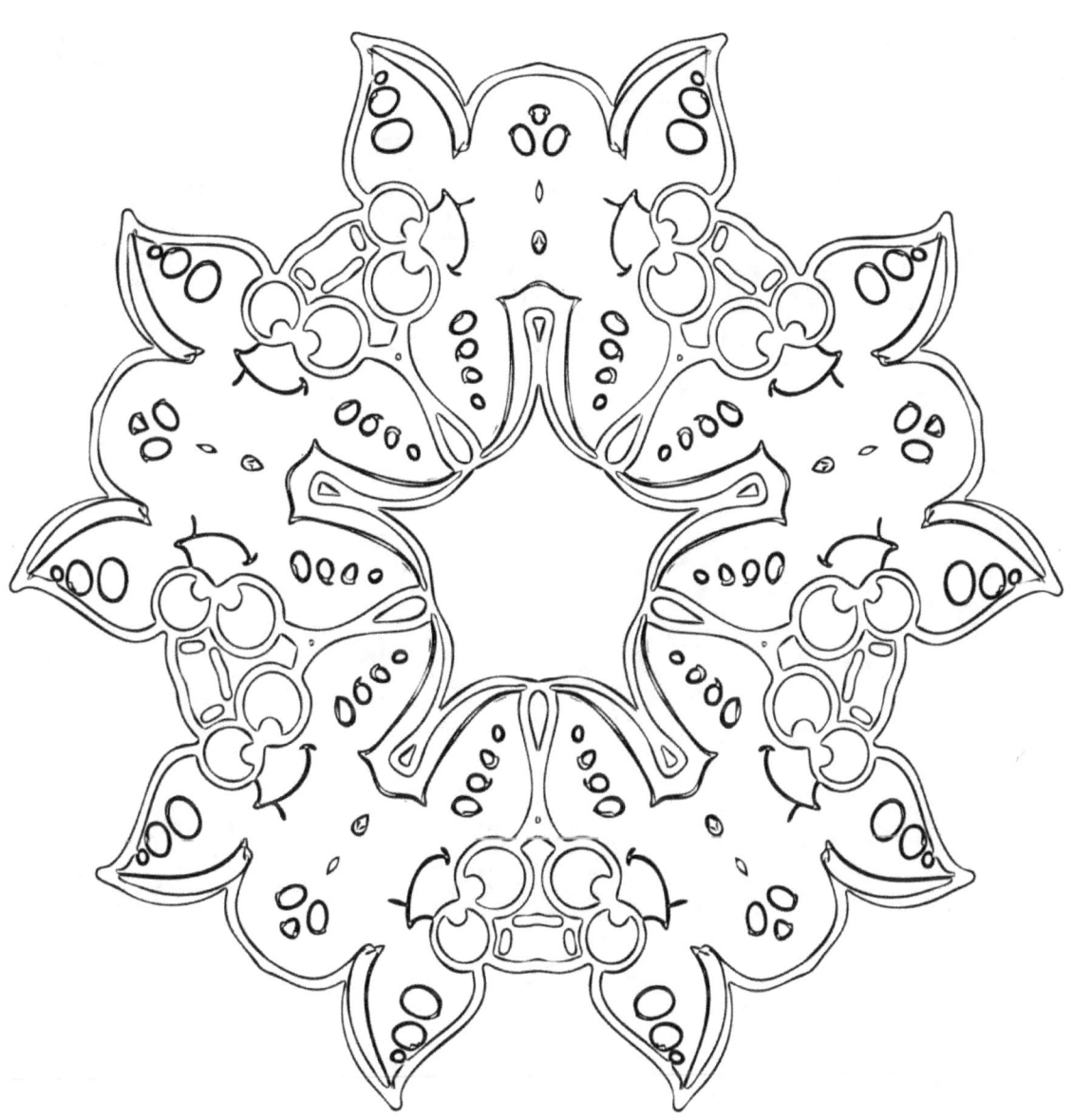

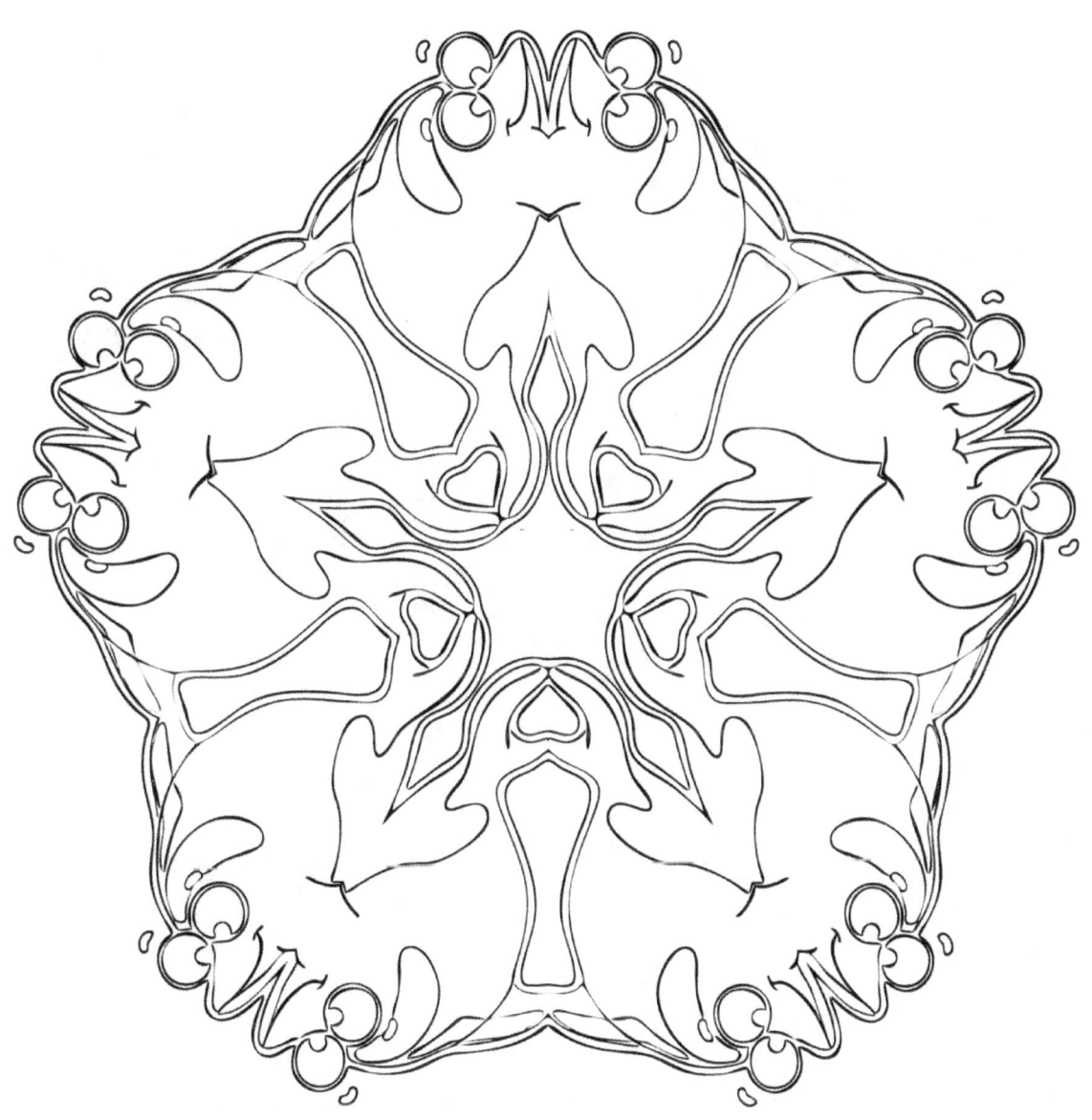

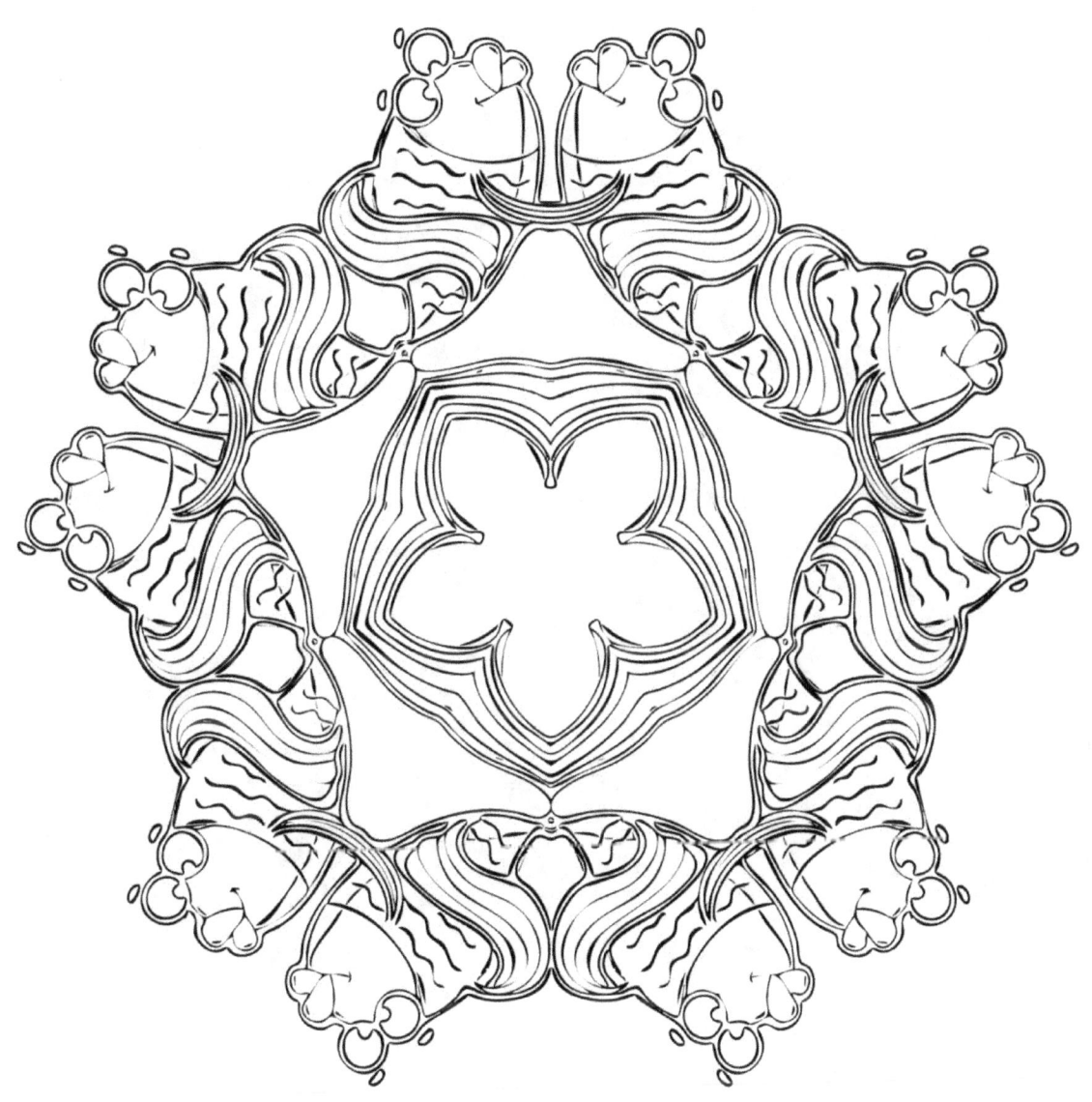

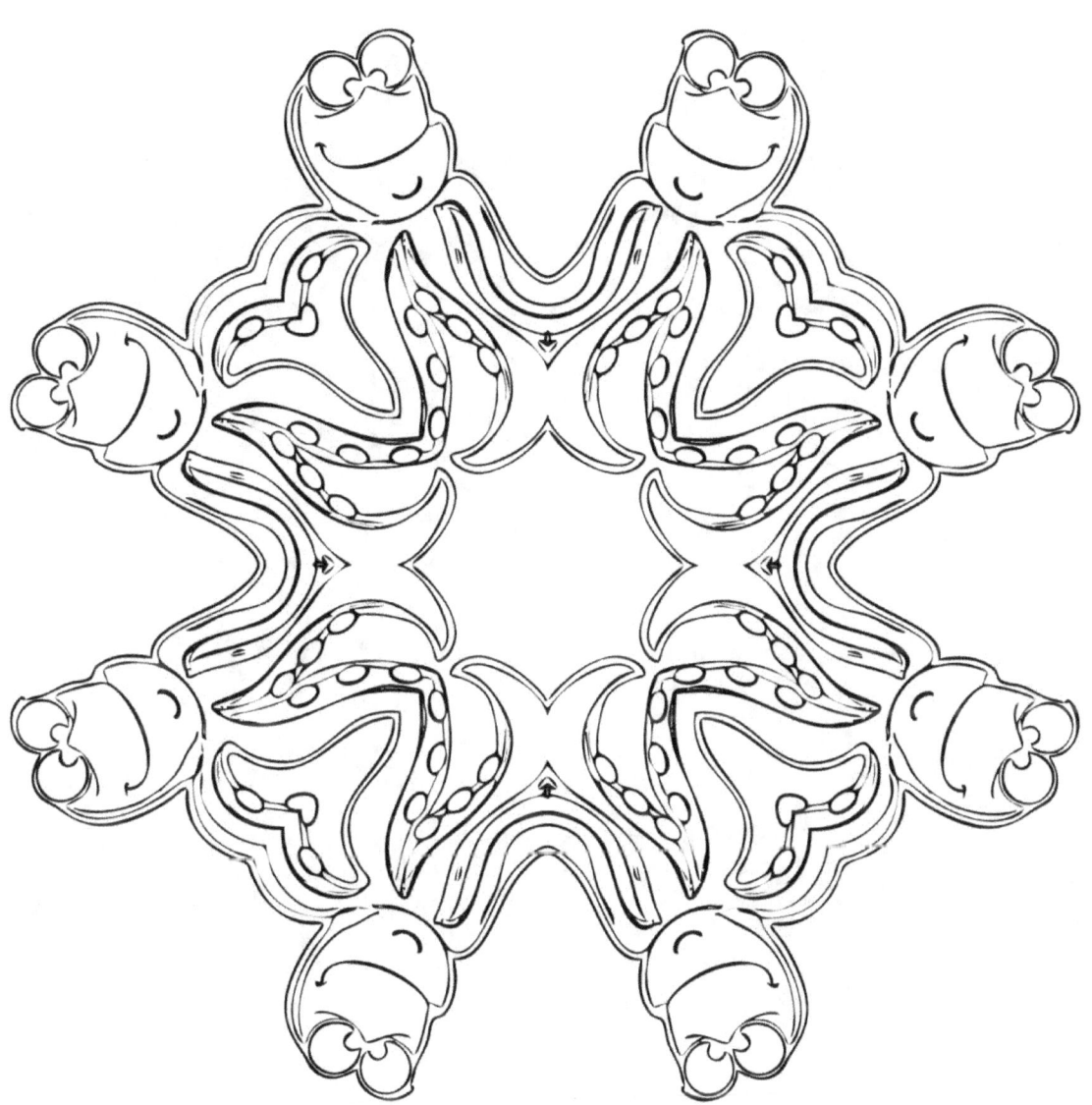

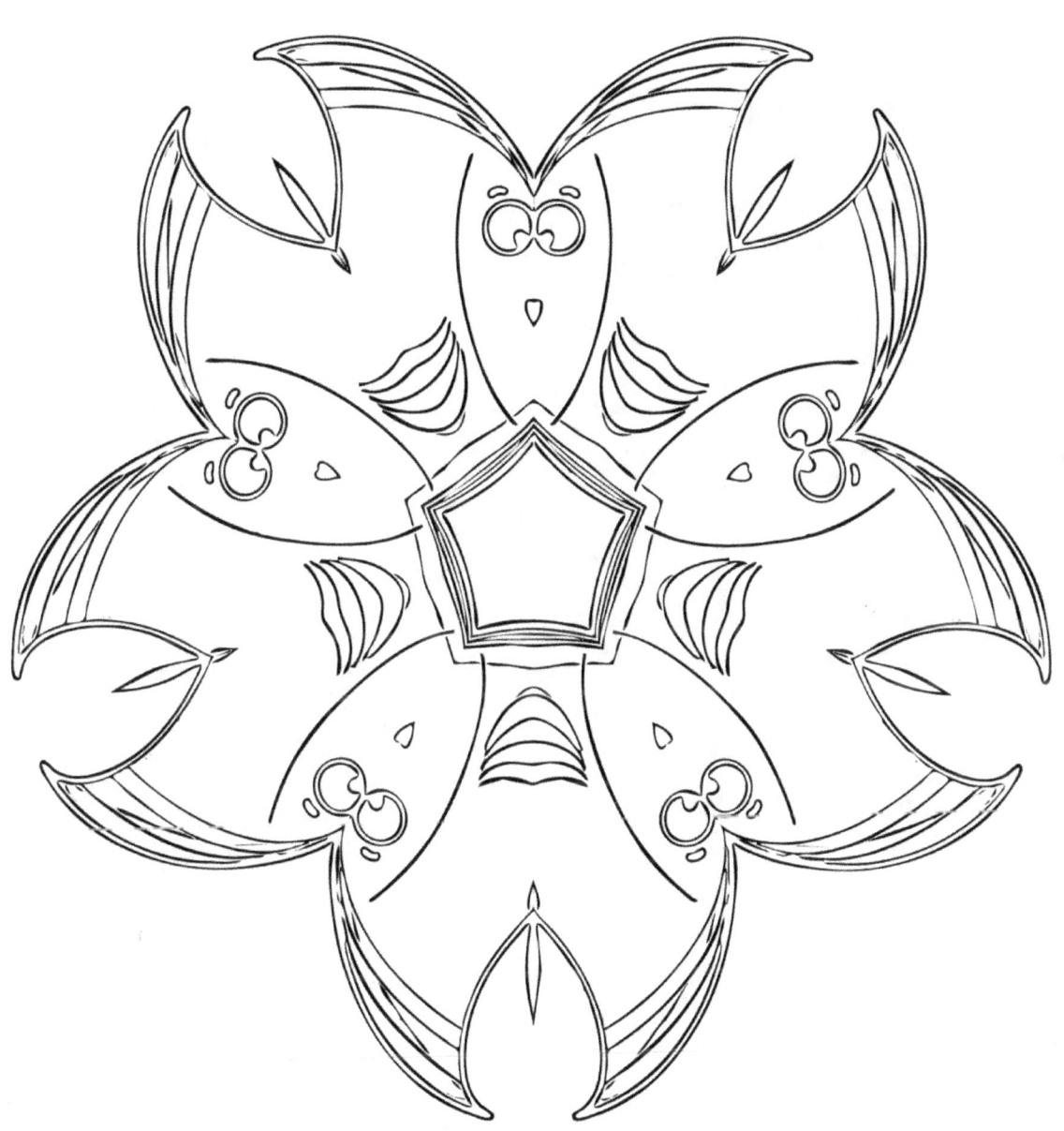

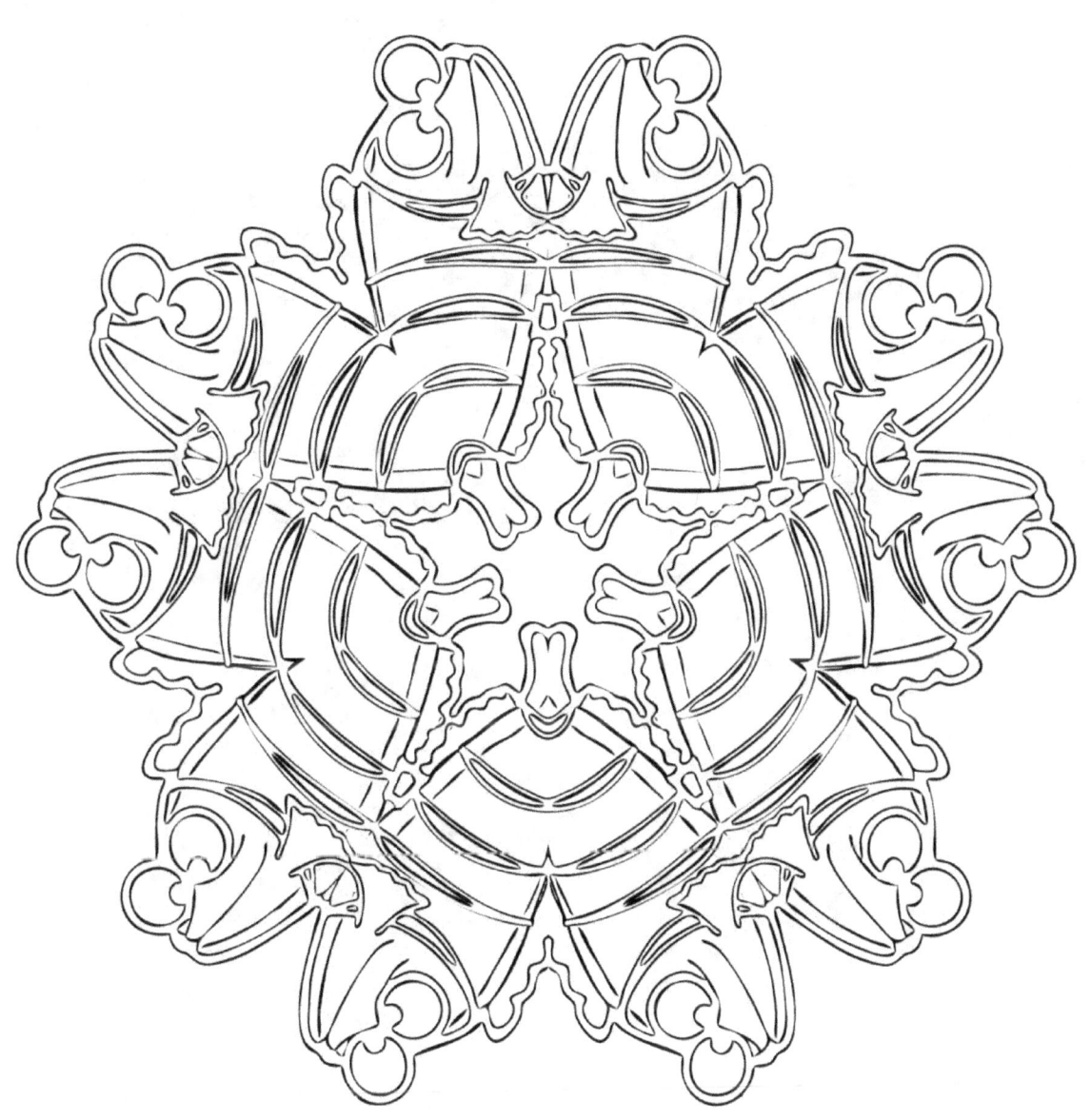

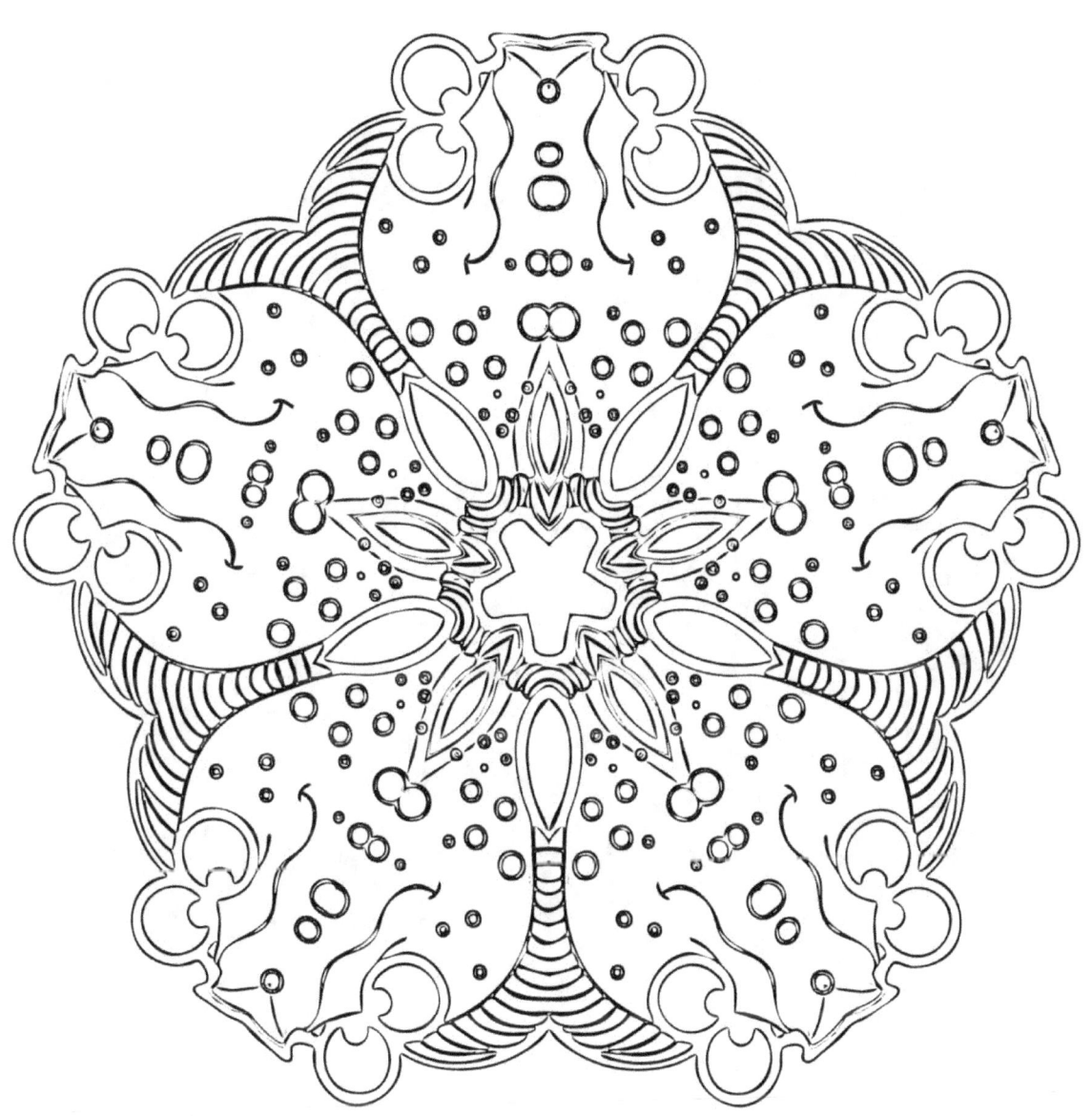

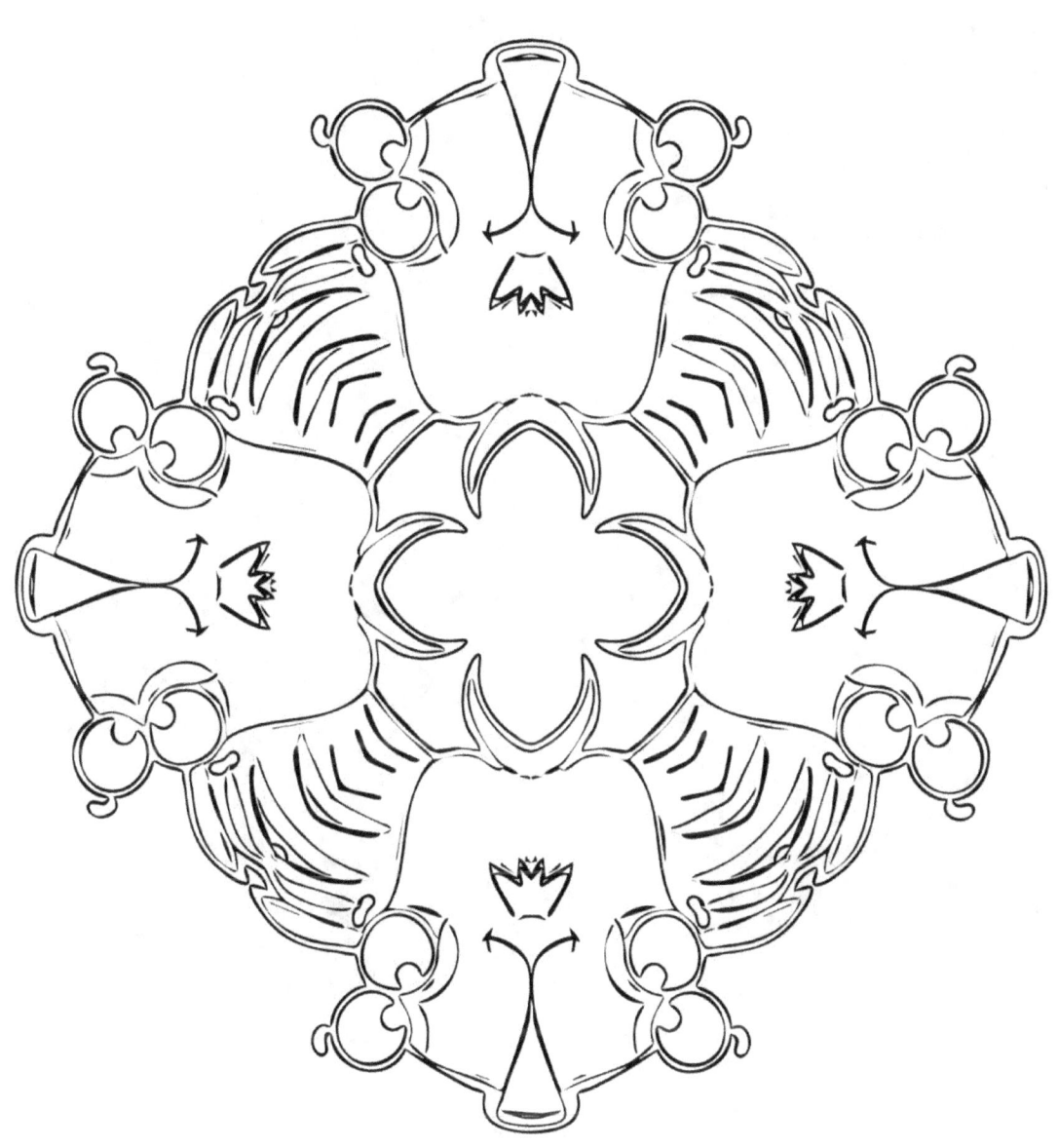

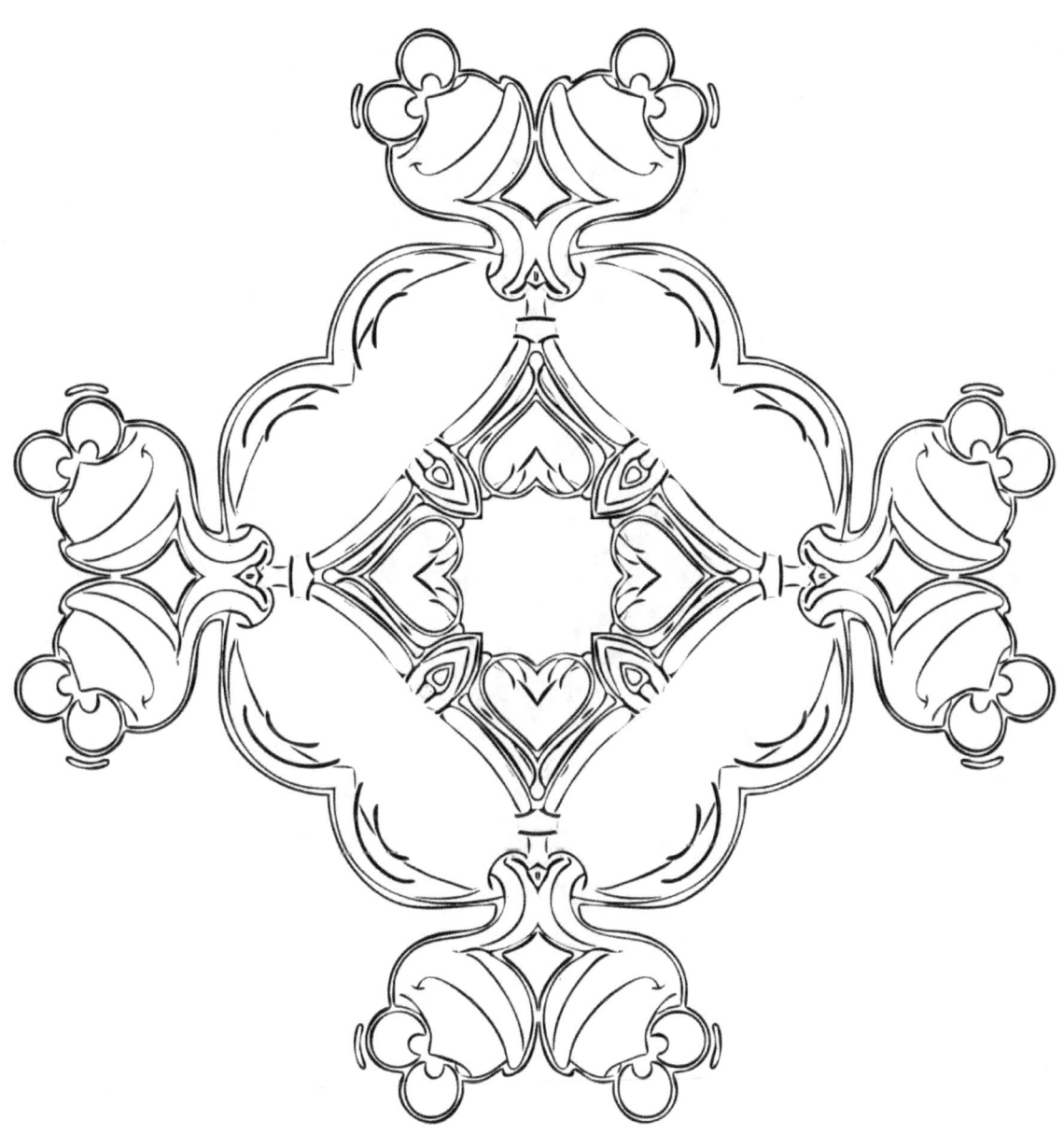

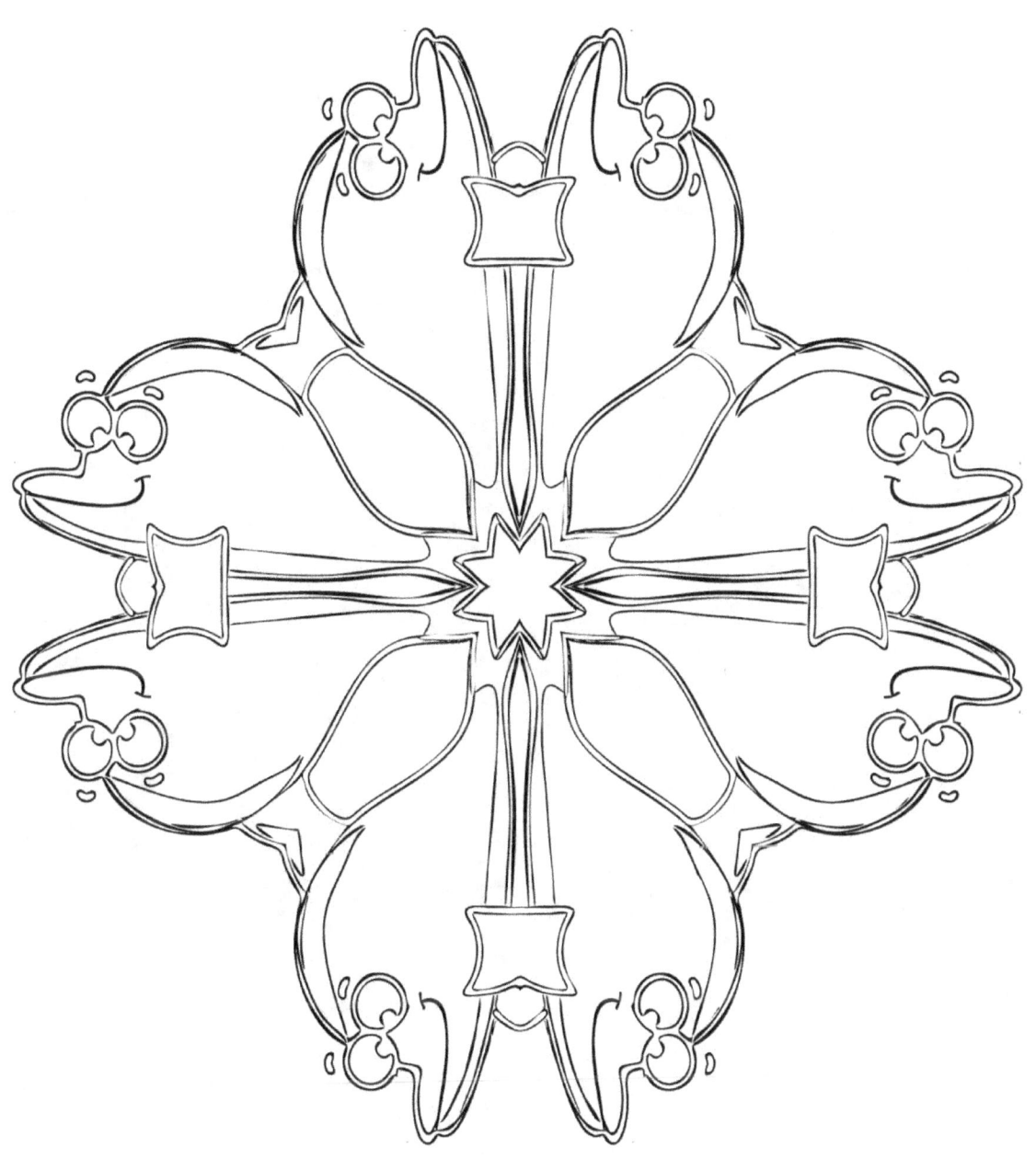

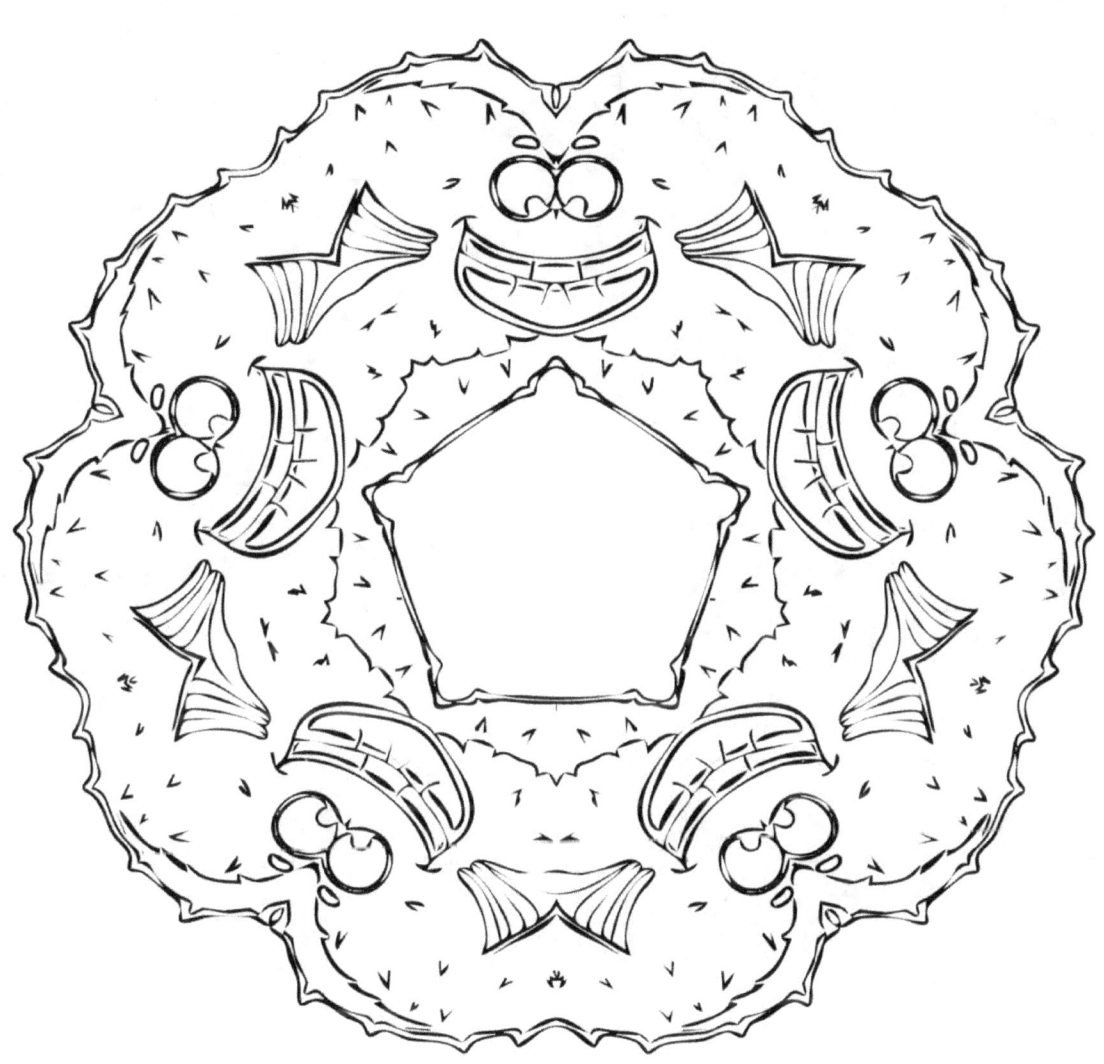

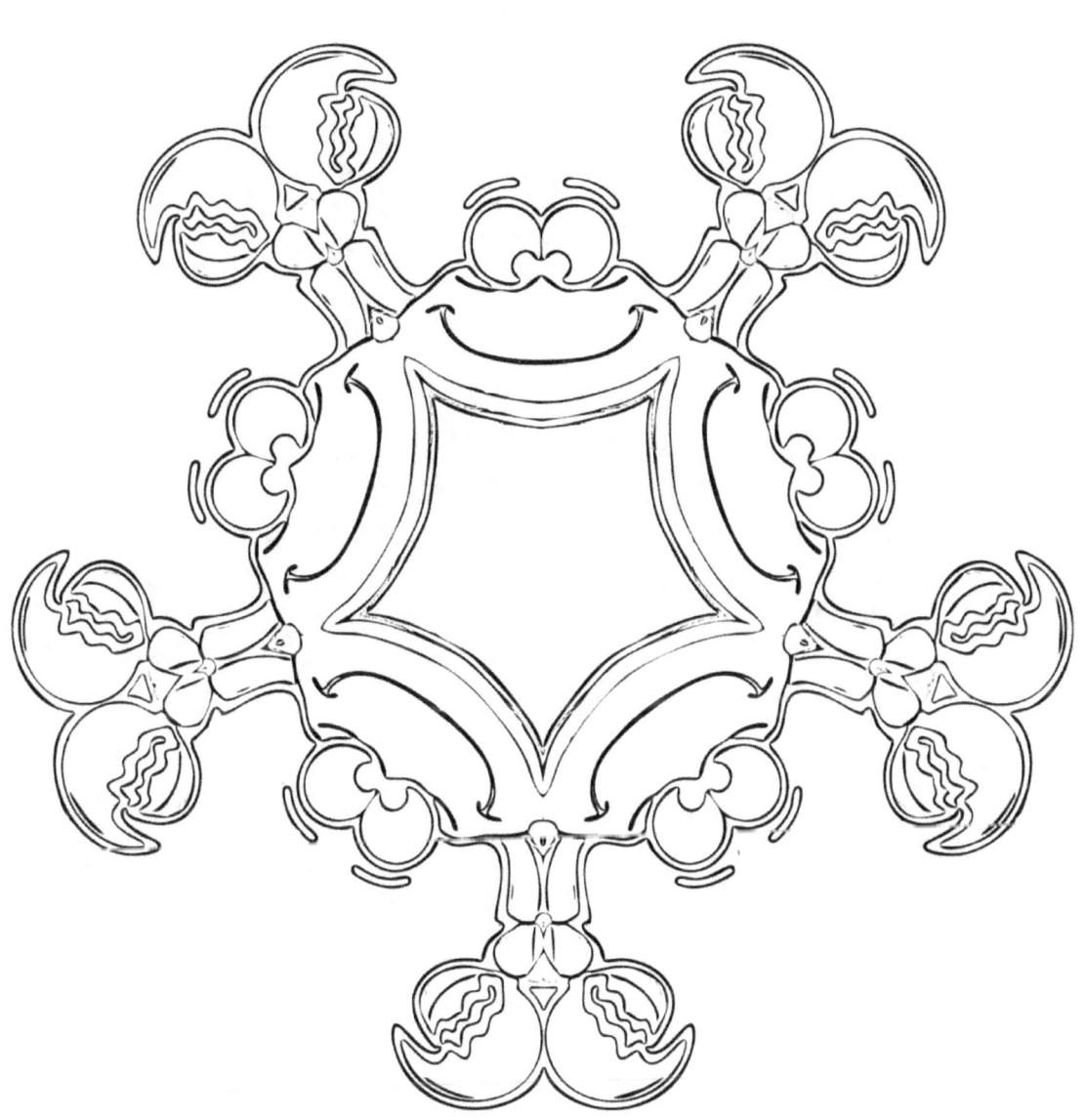

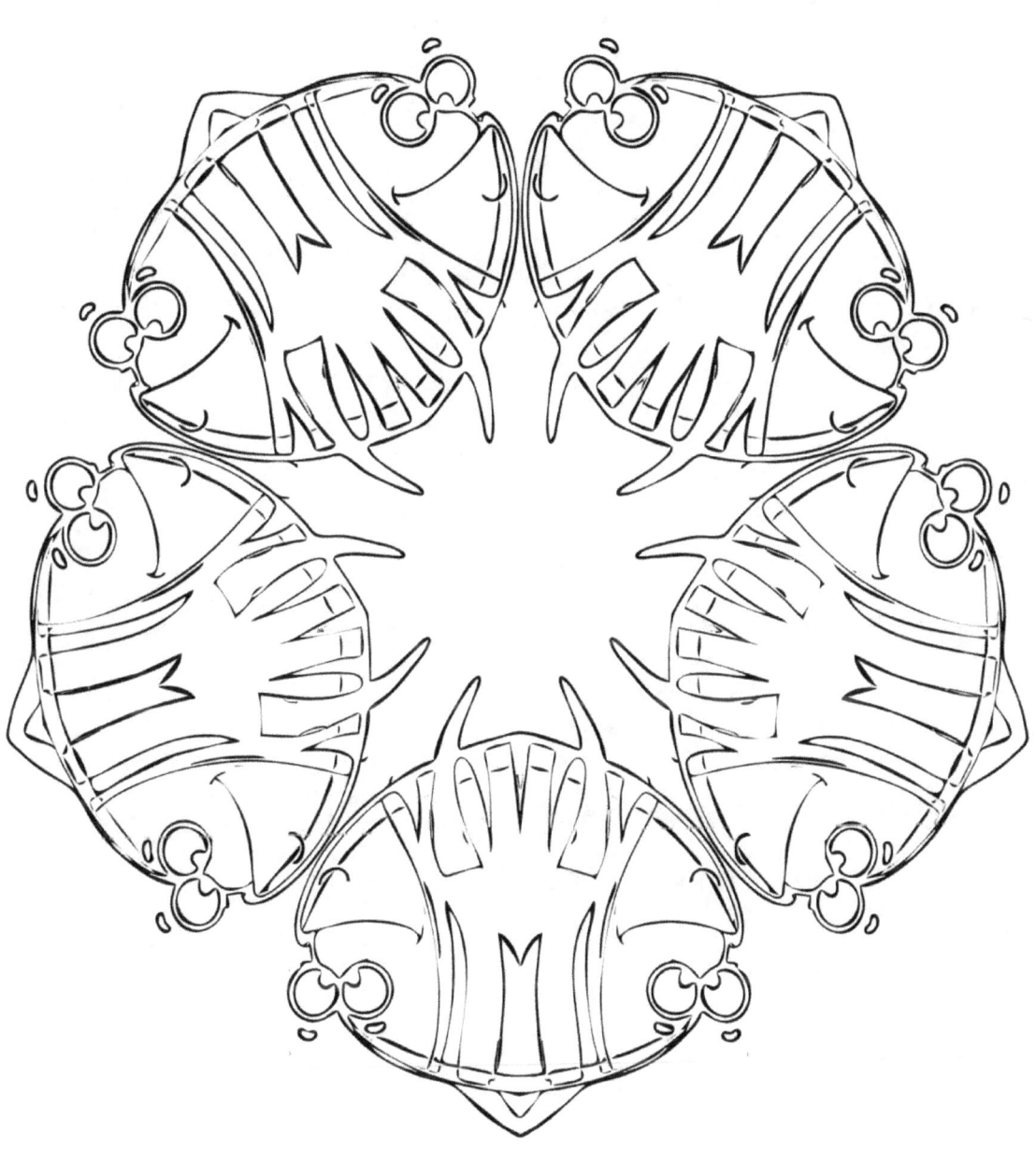

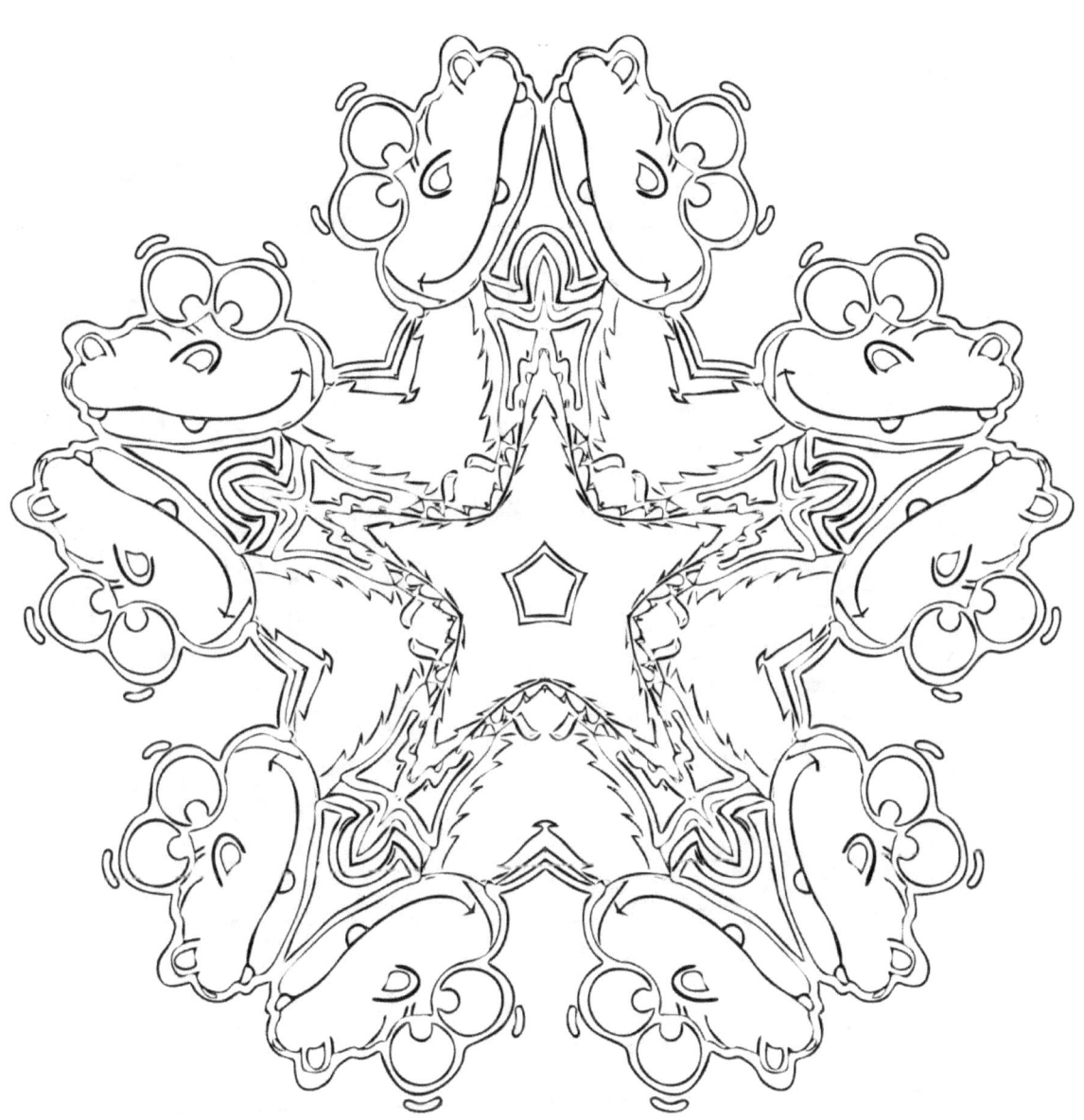

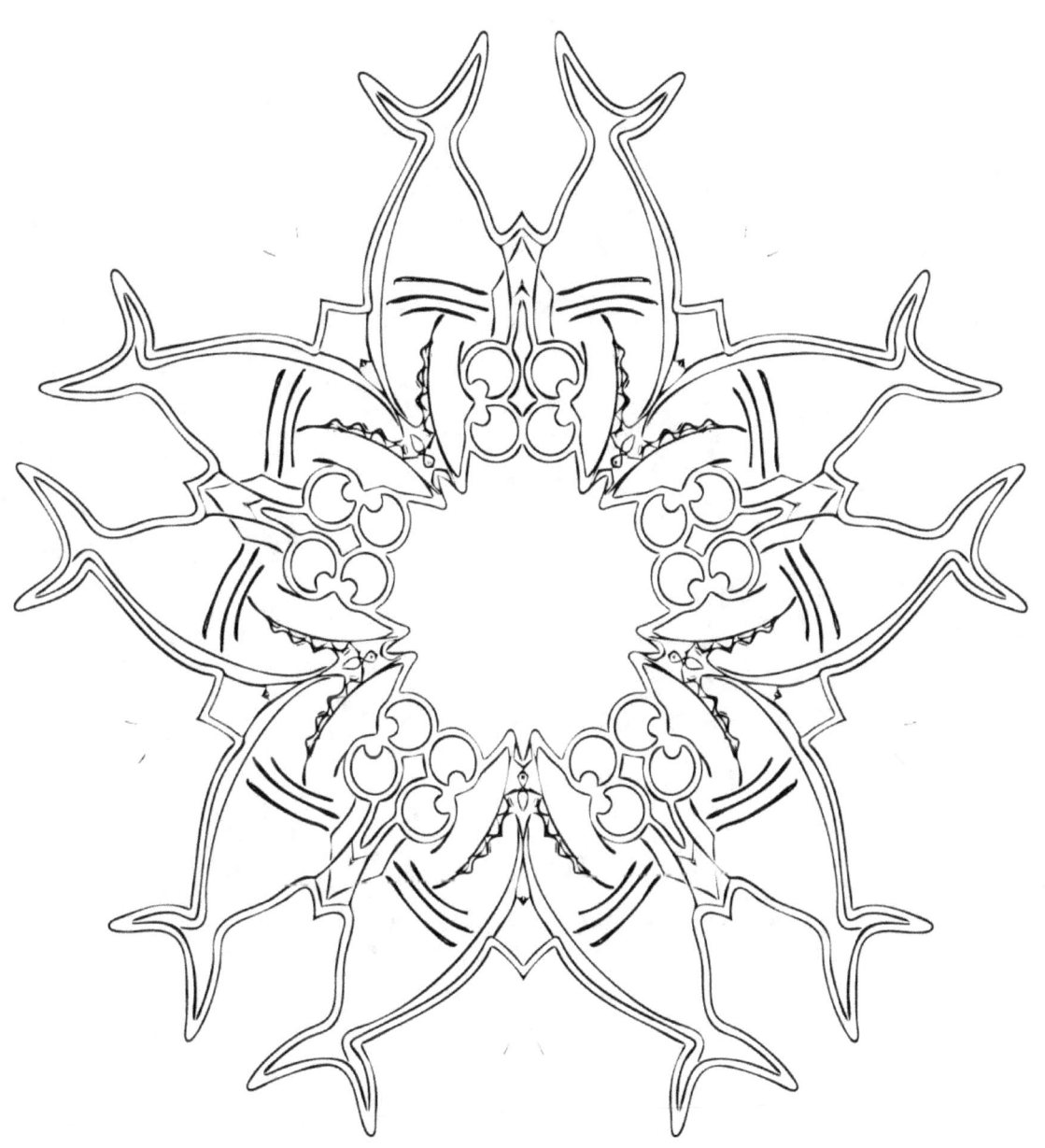

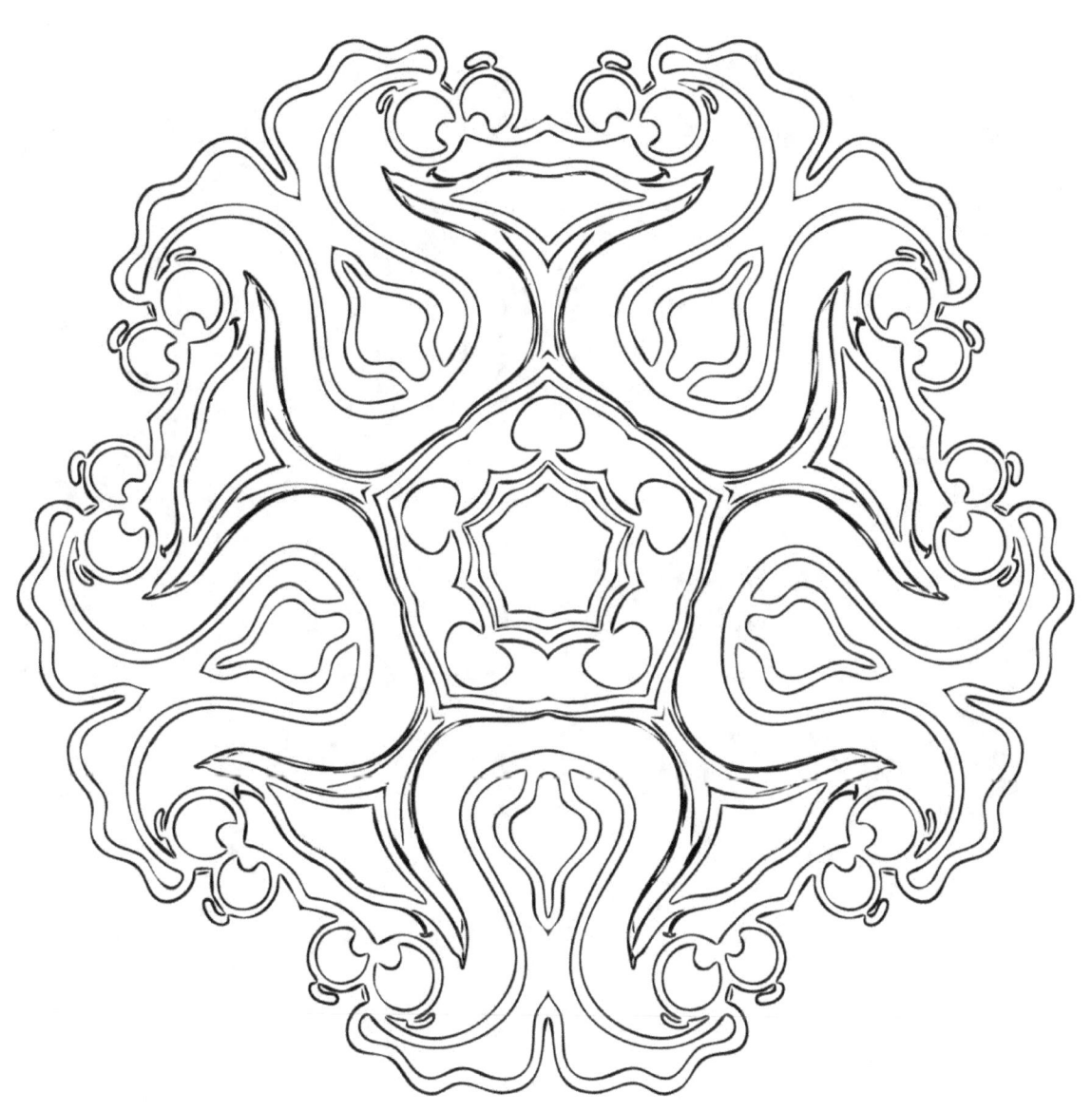

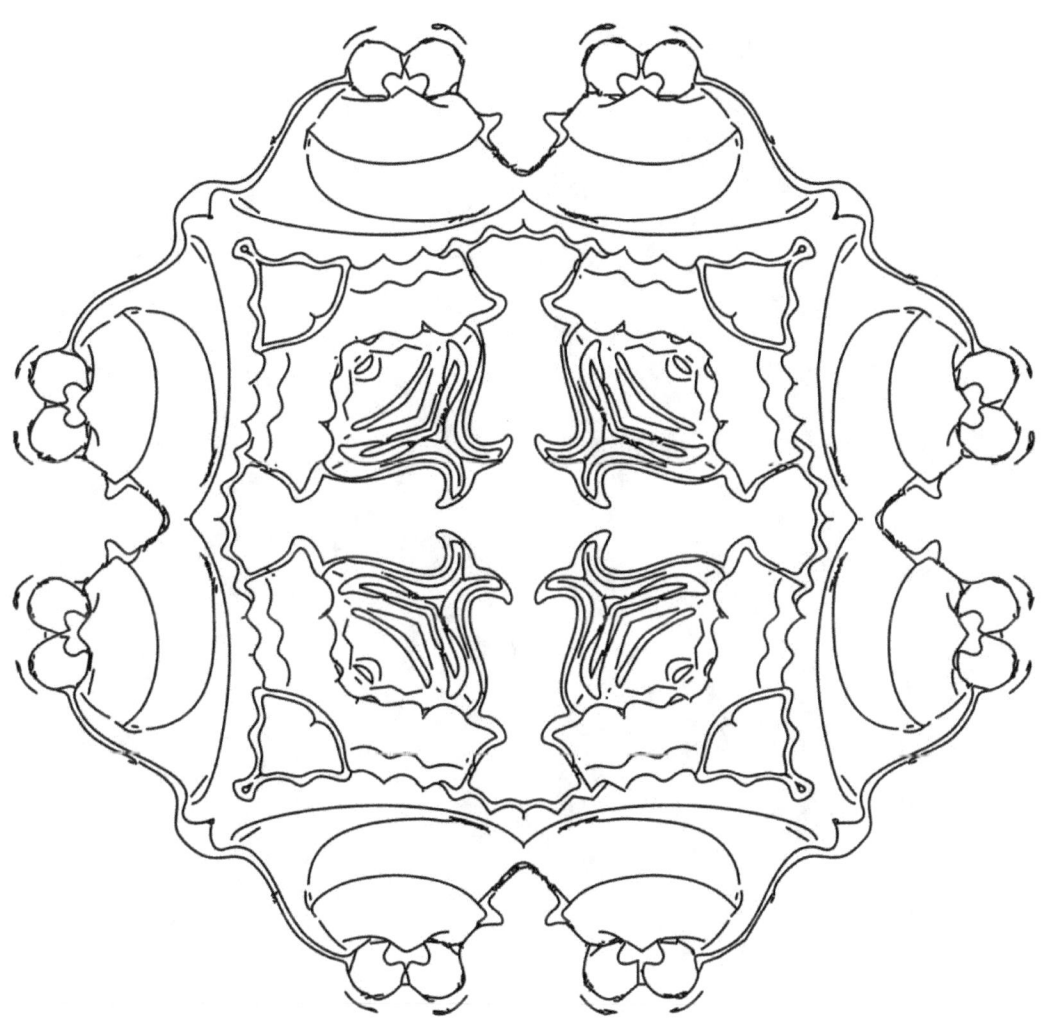

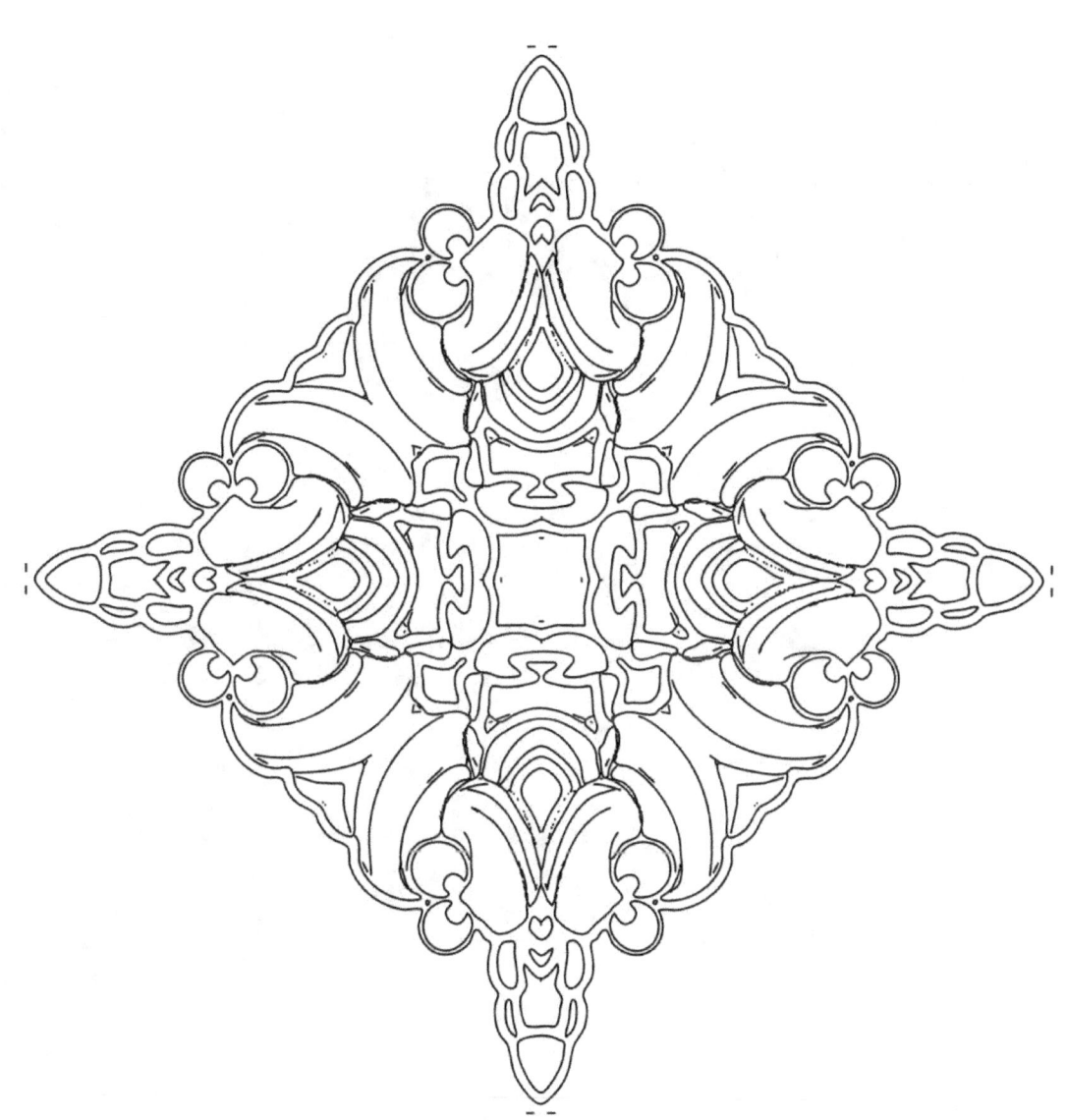

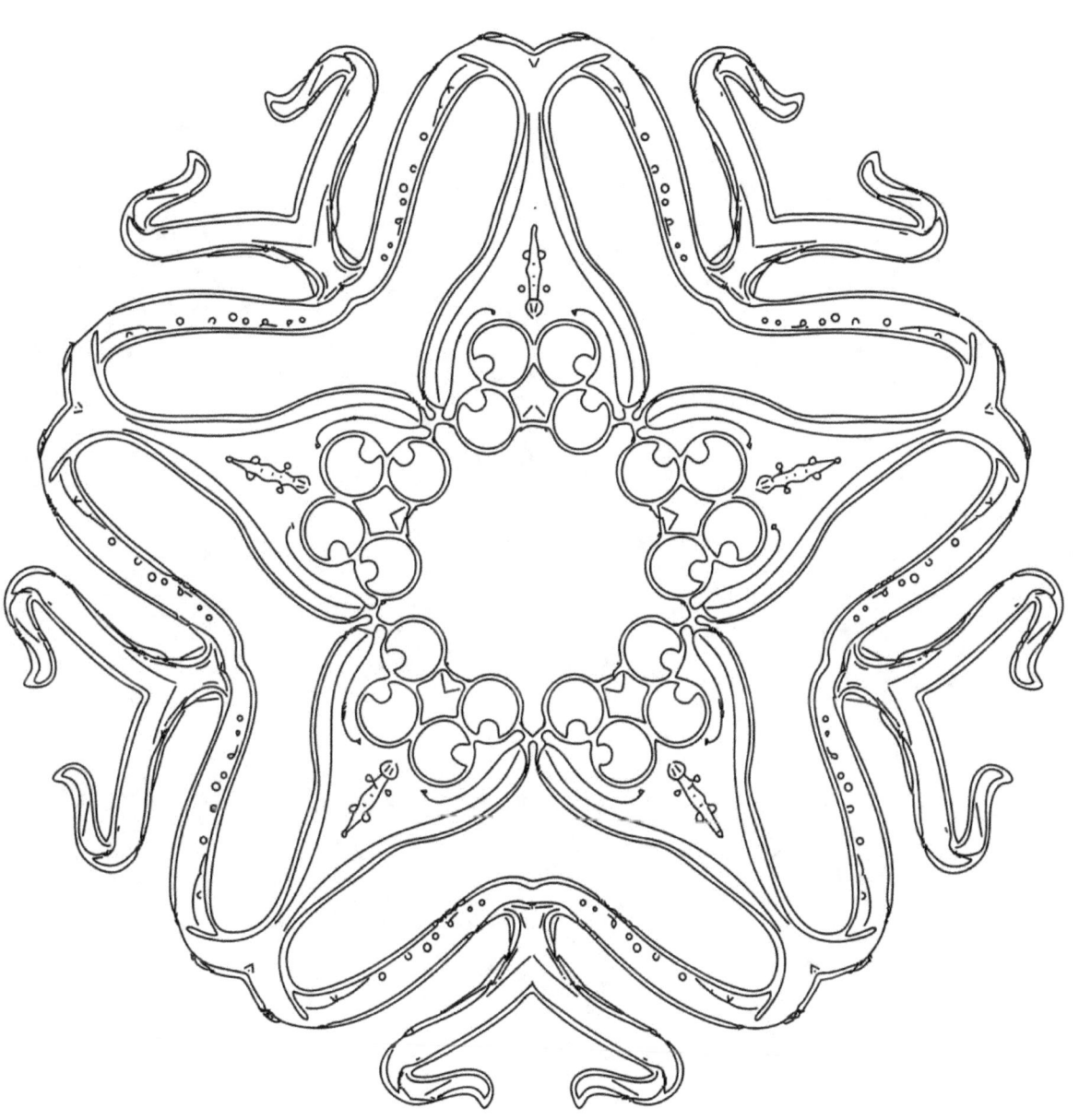

Ocean Coloring Book

PSYCHEDELIC STRESS-RELIEVING FISH 2

A Coloring Book For Adults

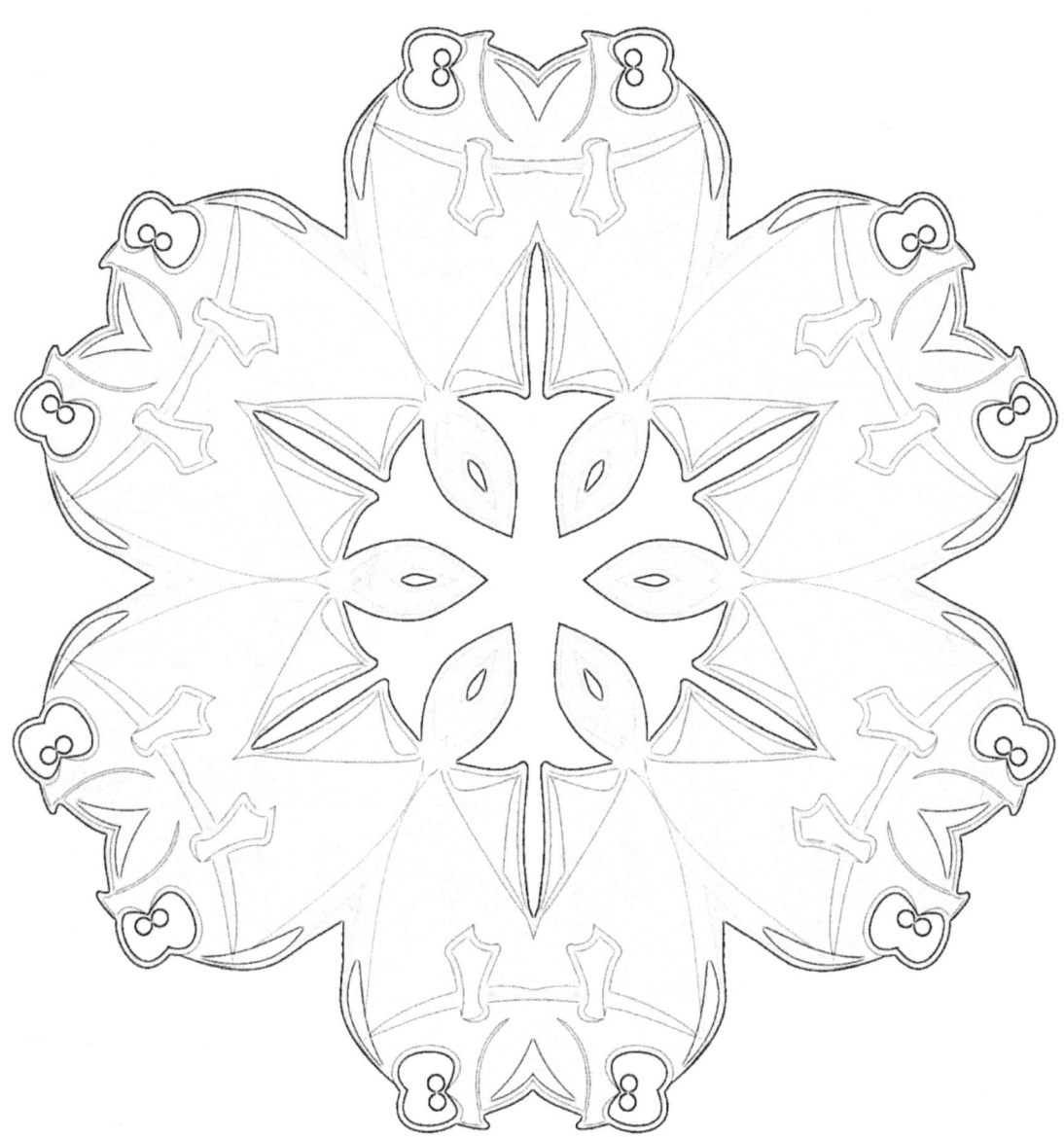

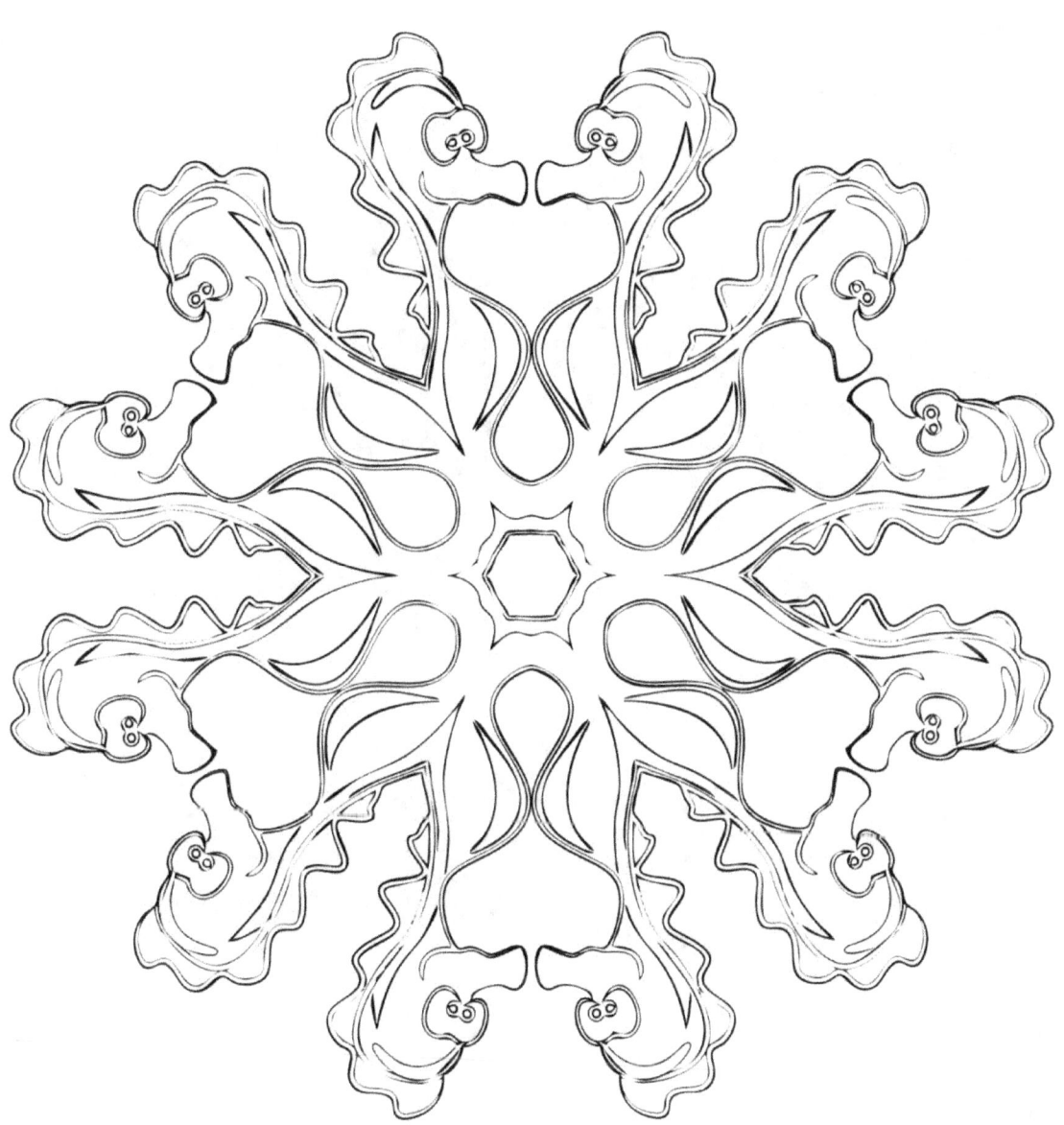

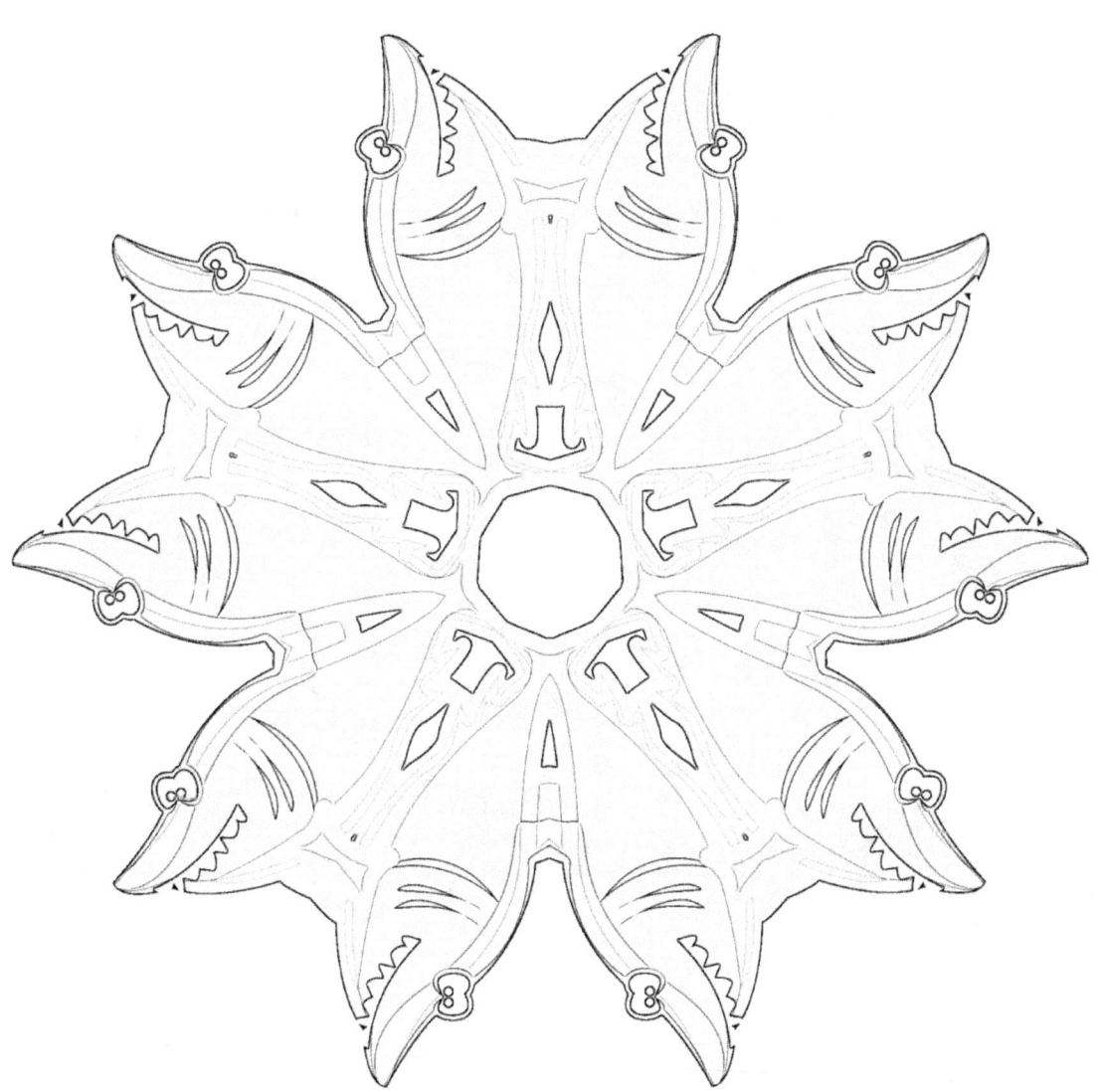

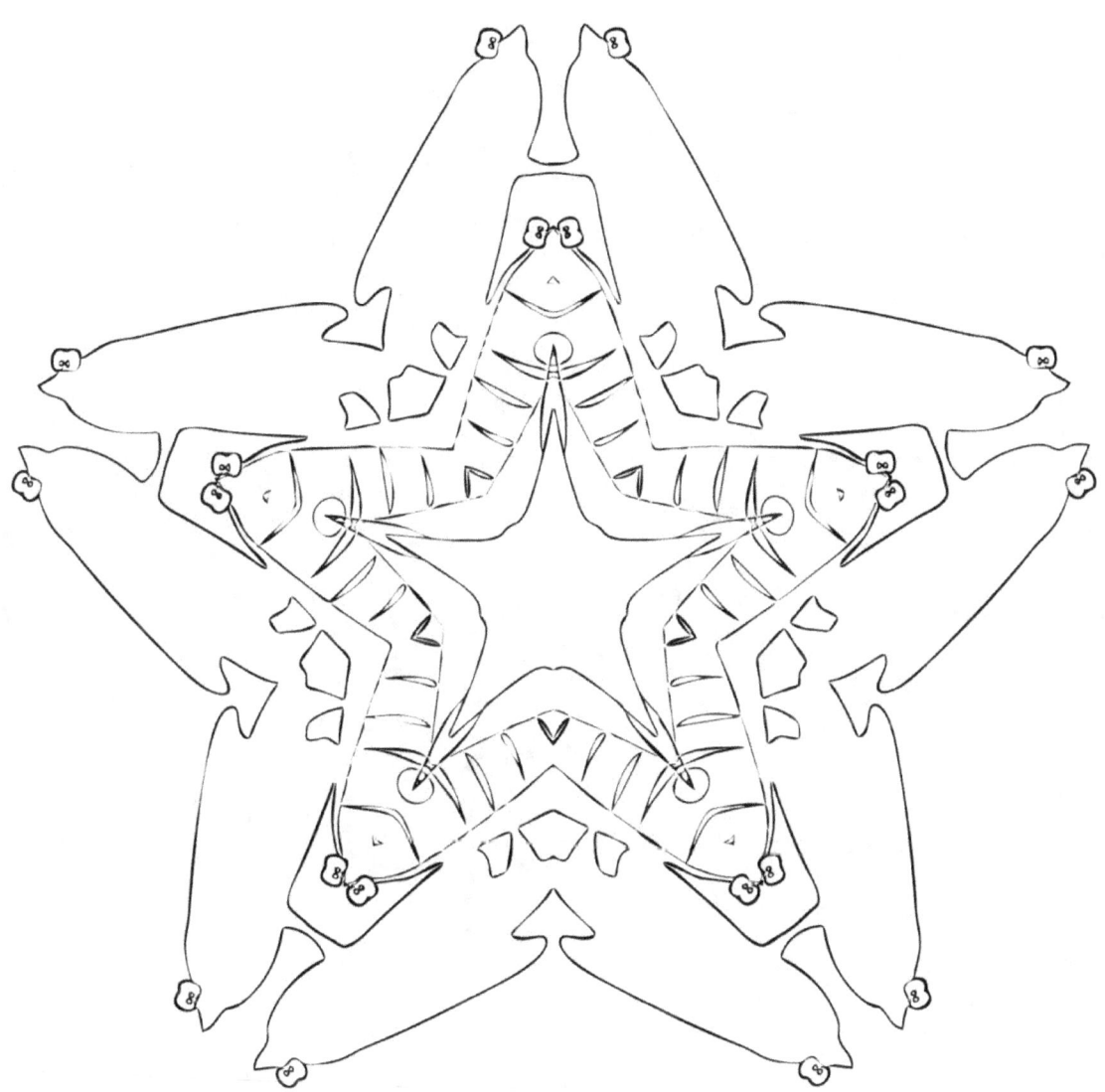

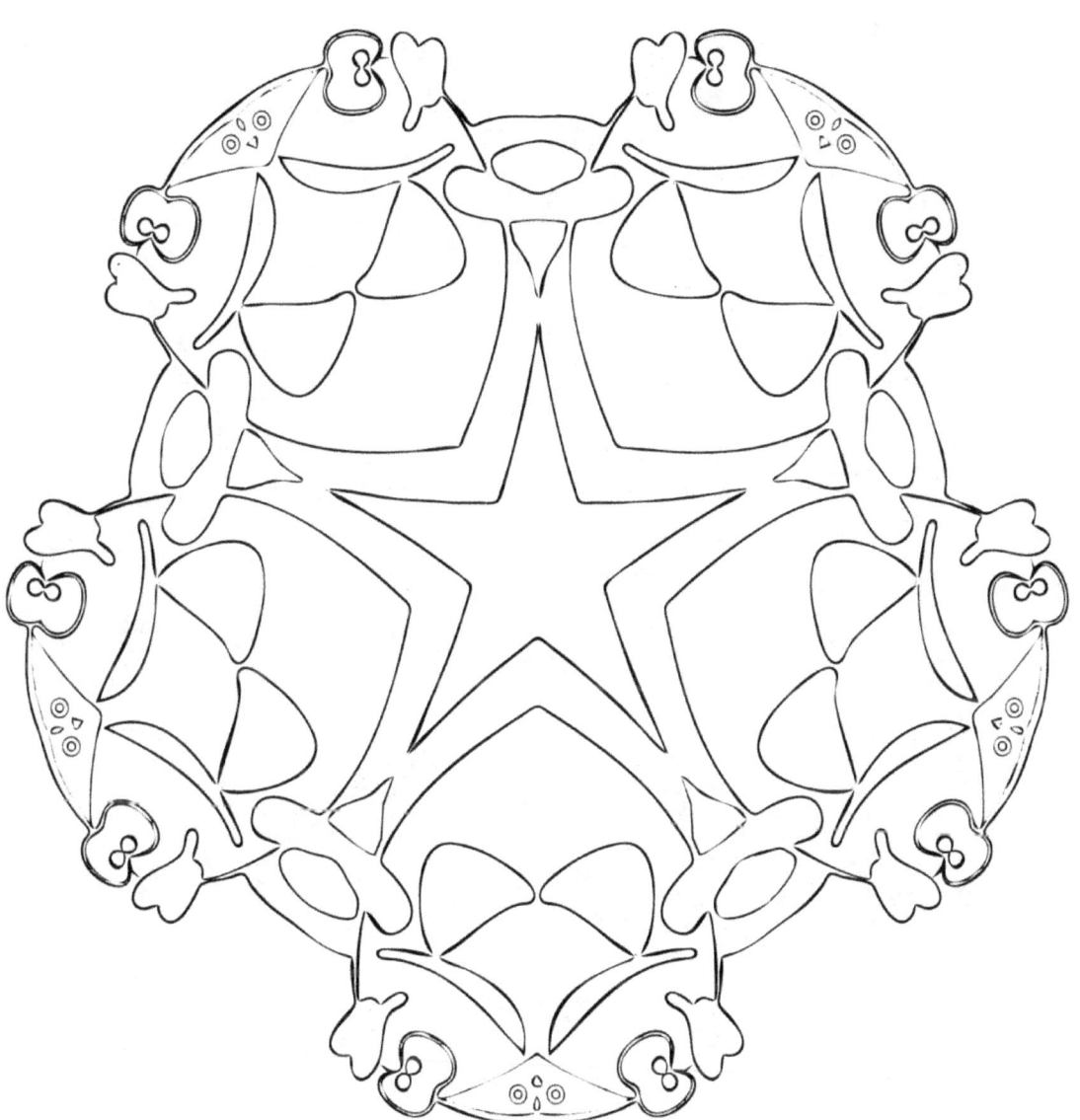

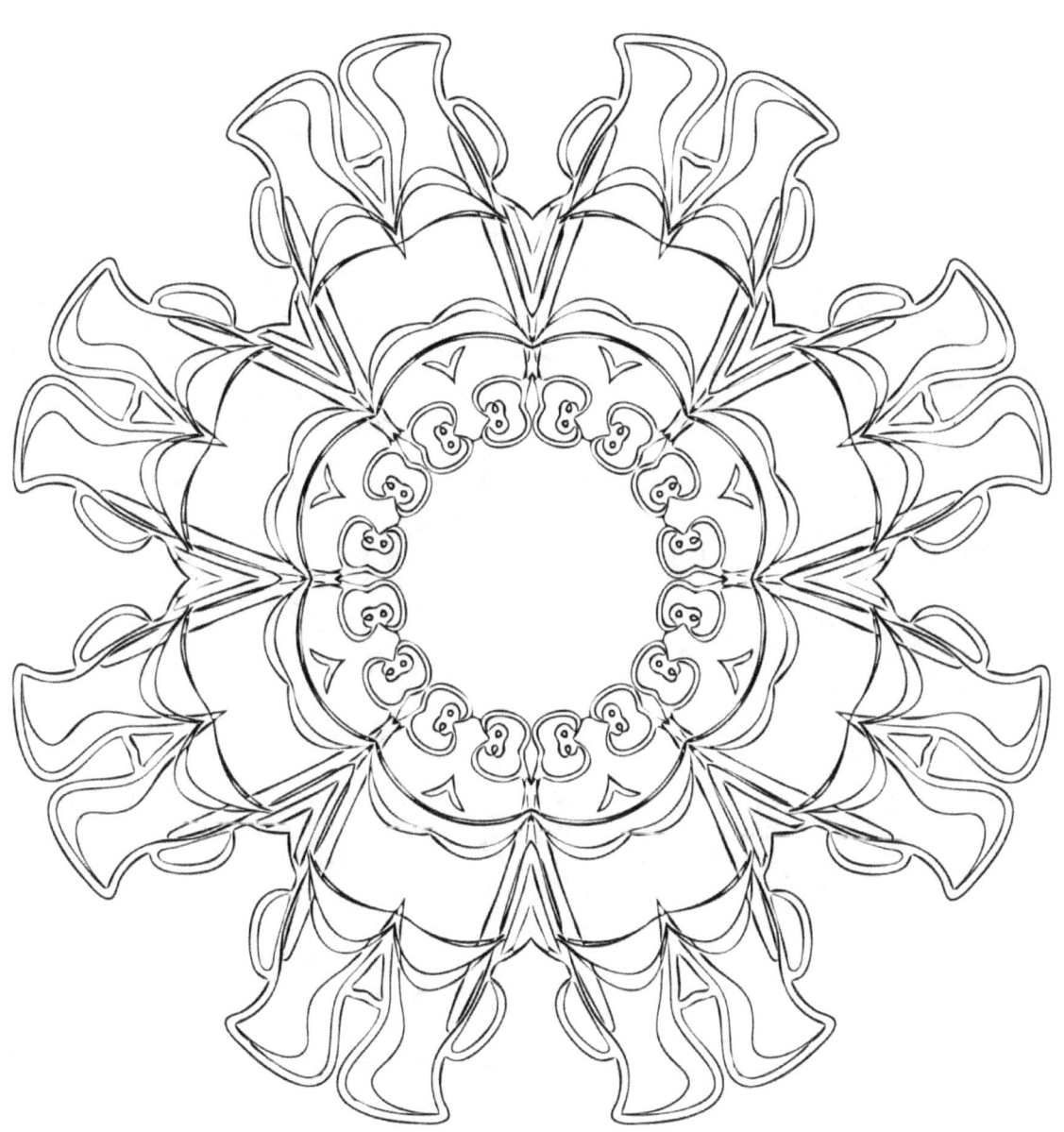

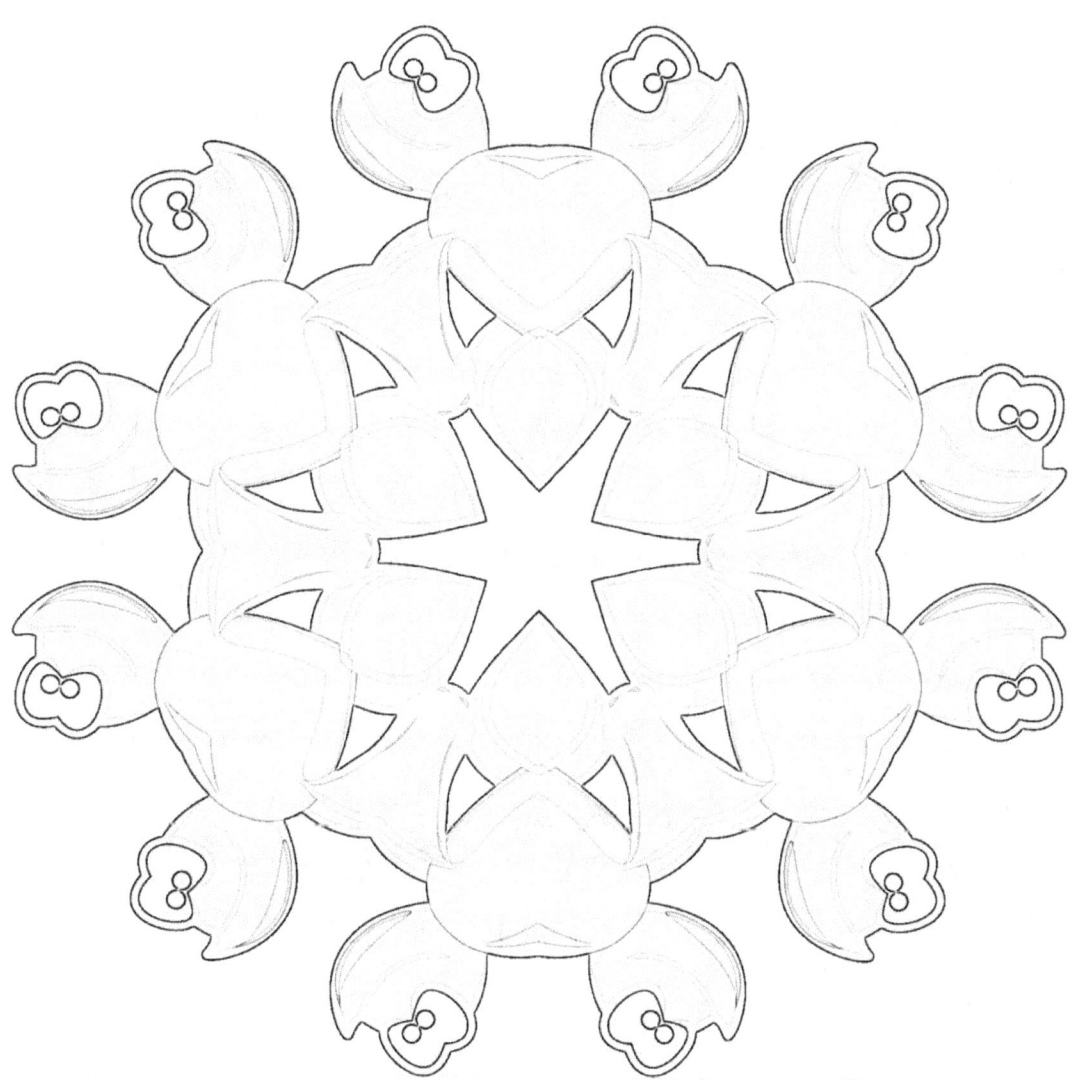

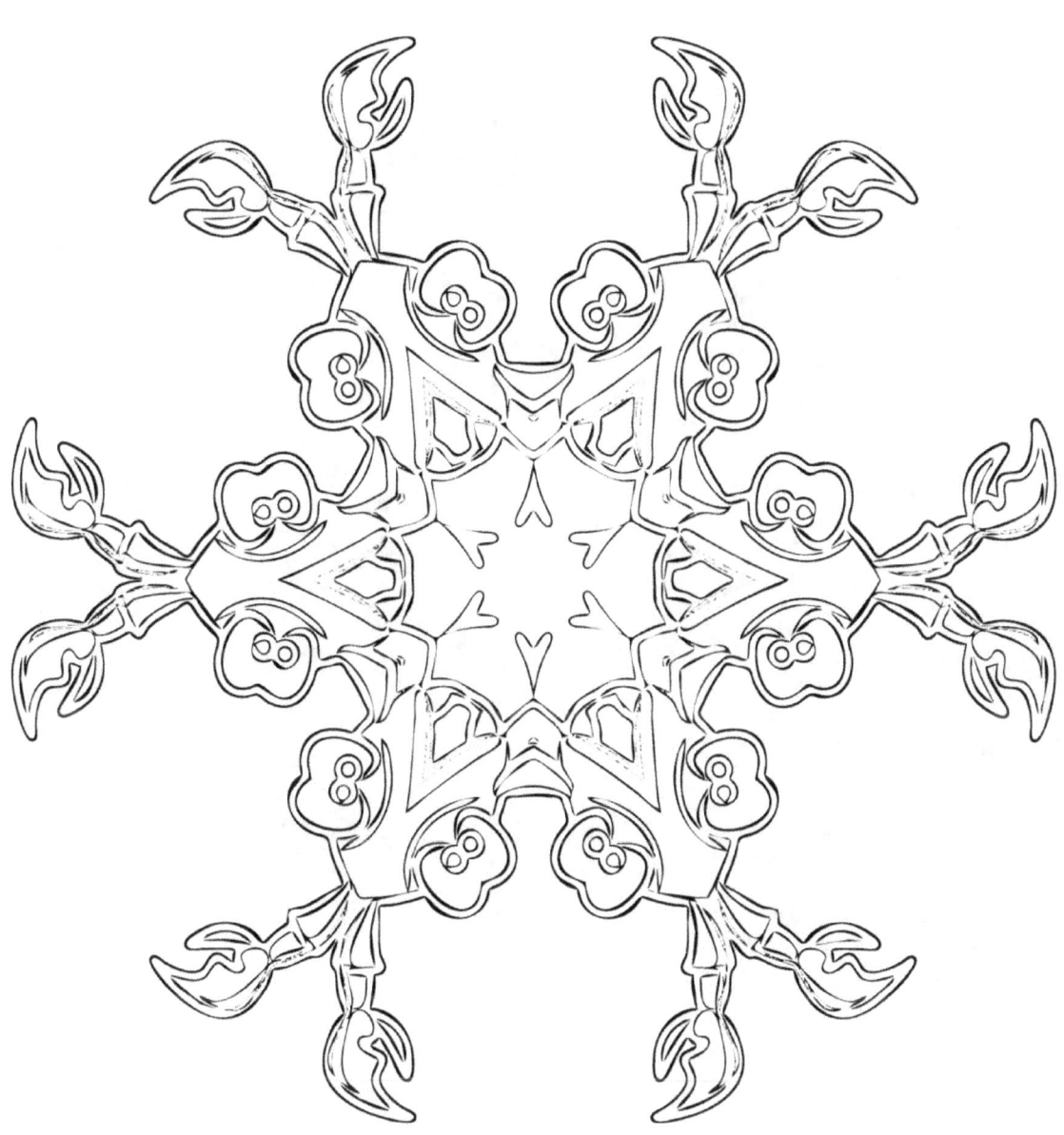

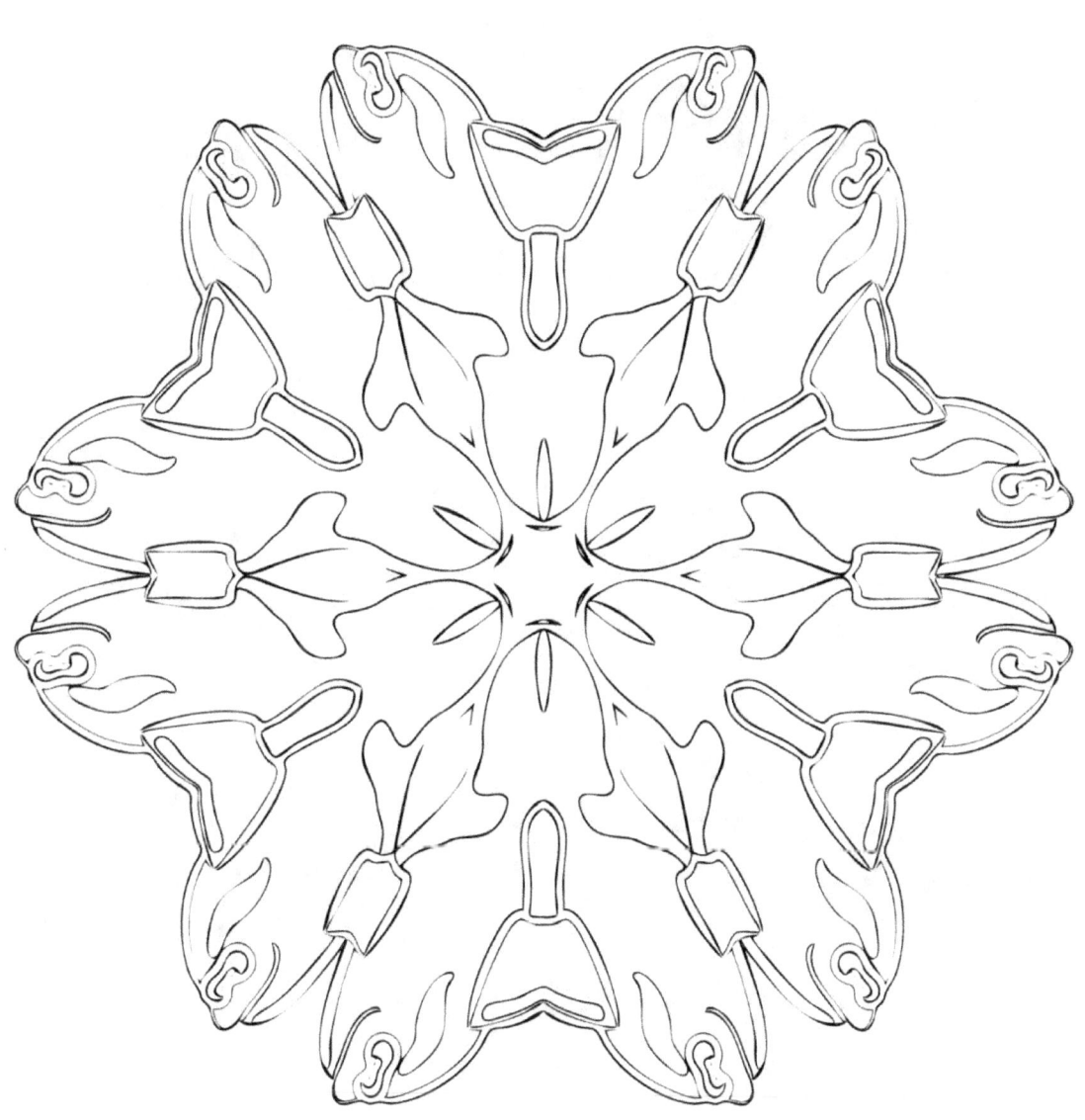

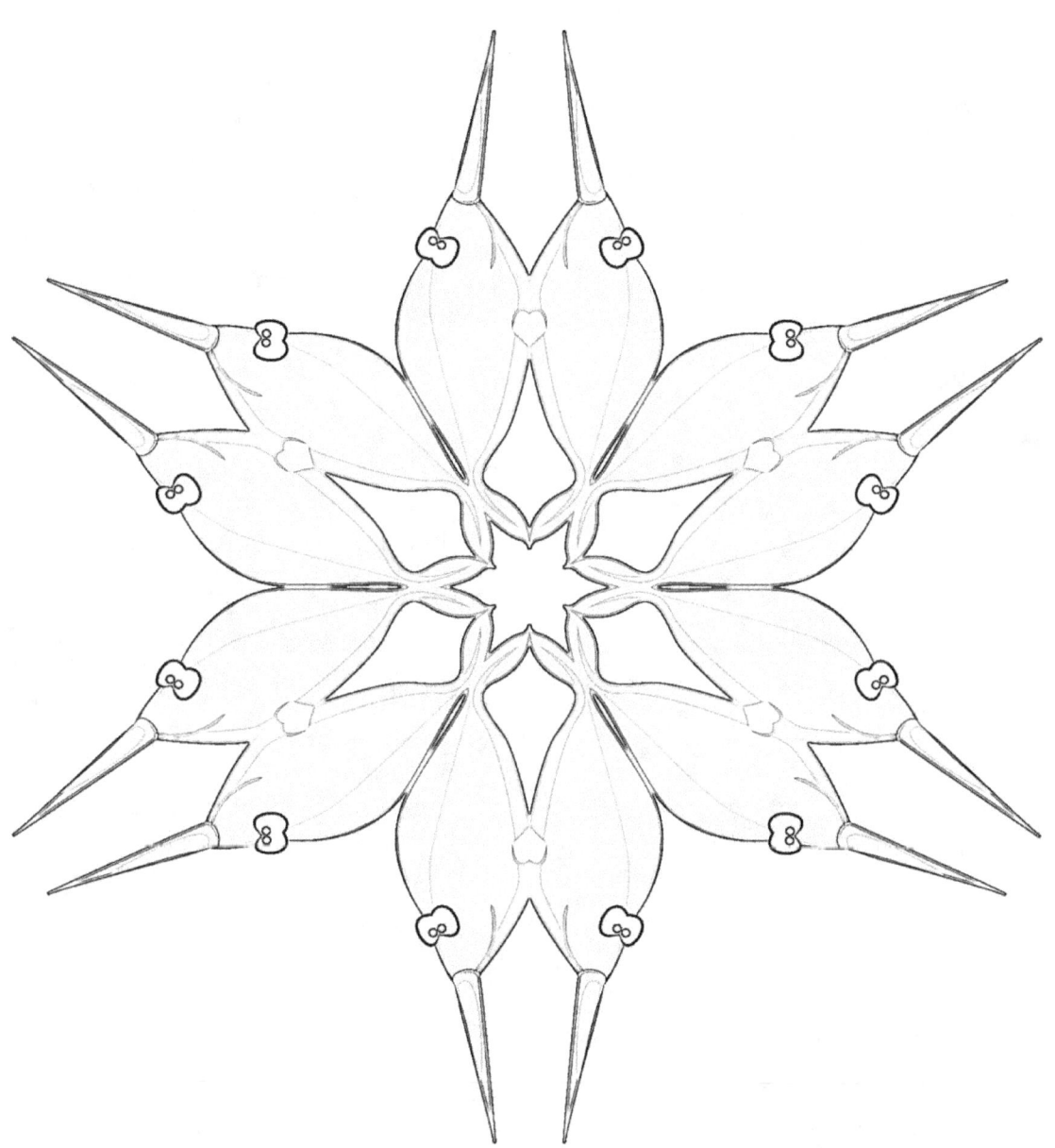

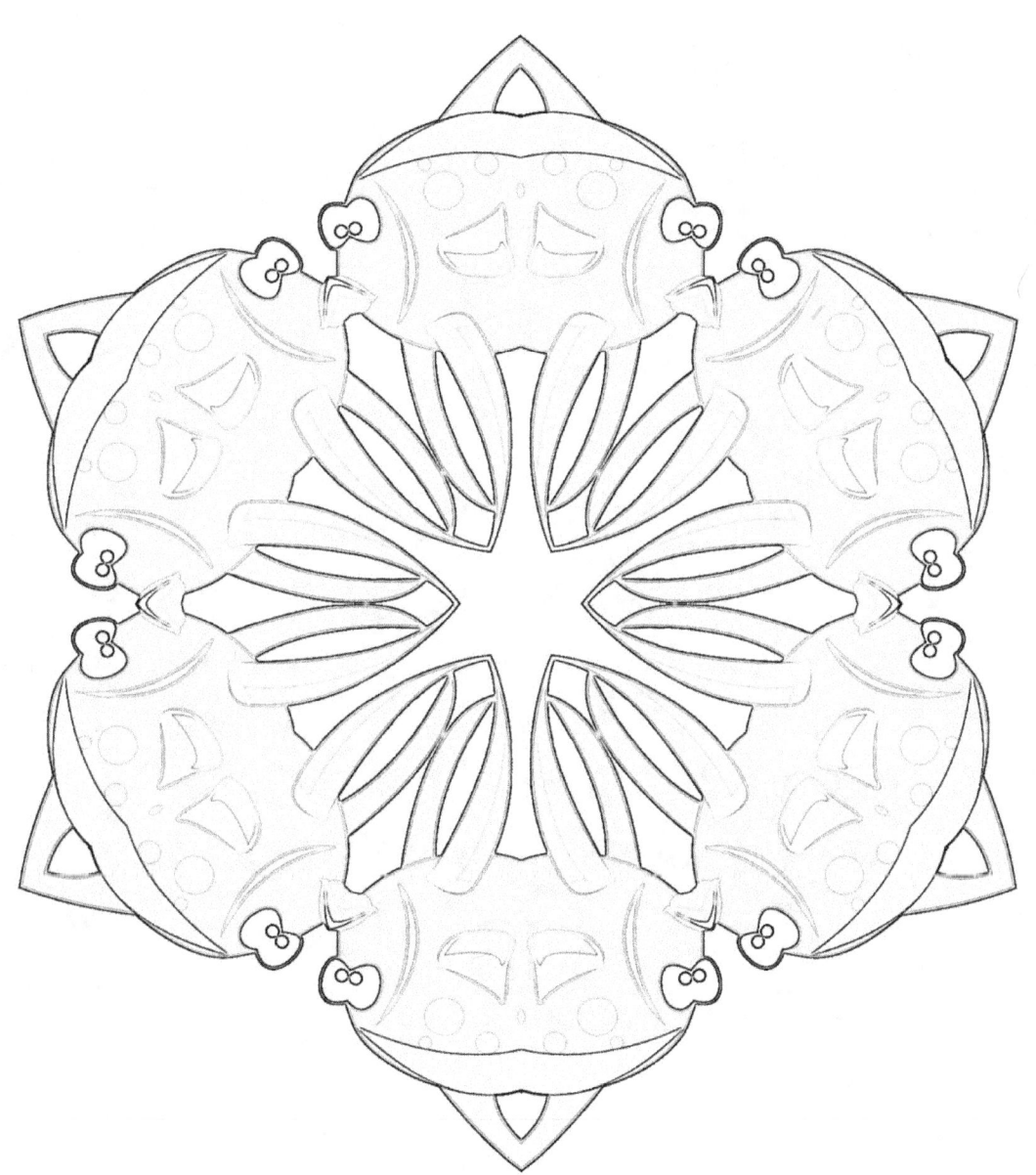

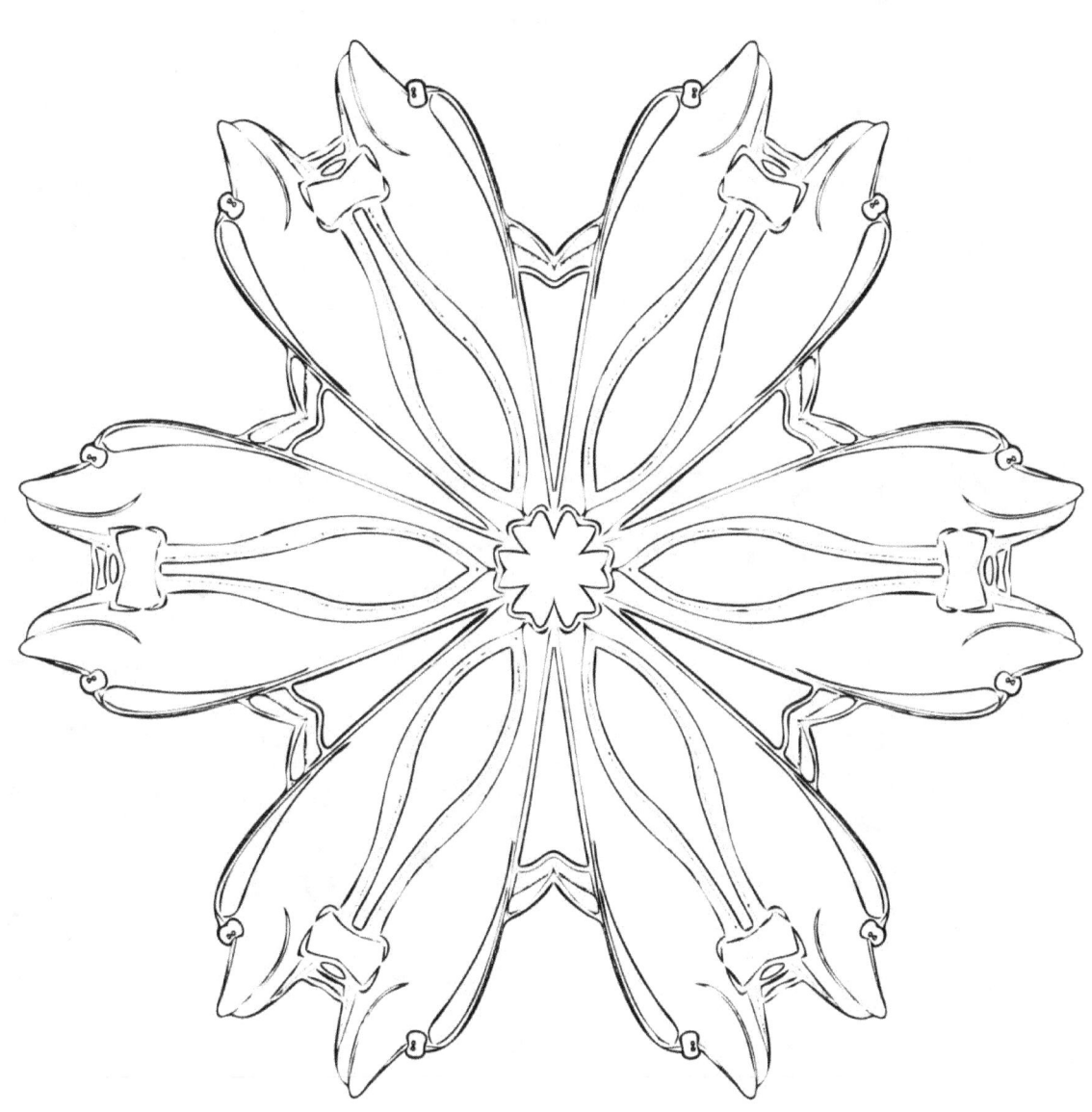

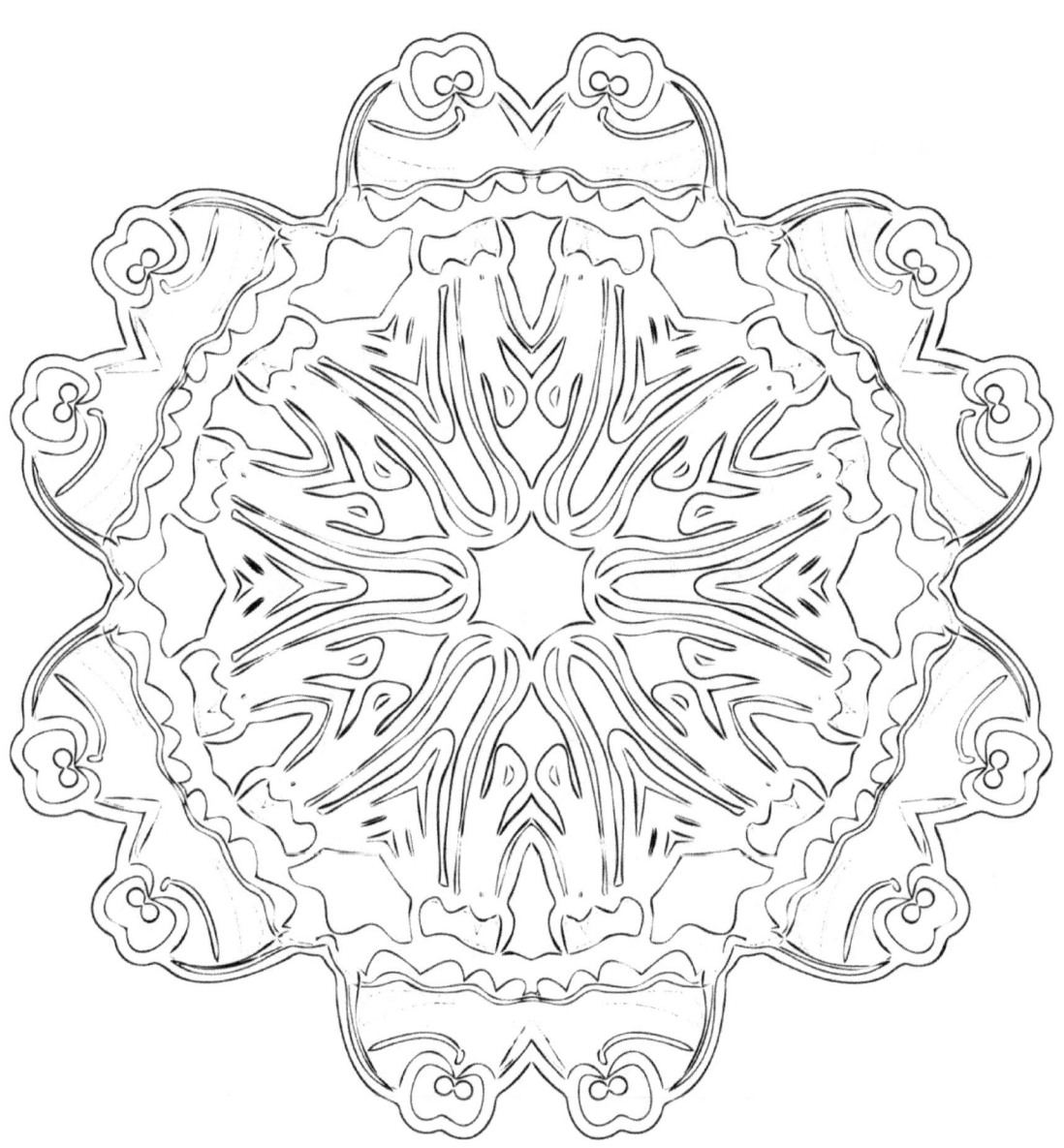

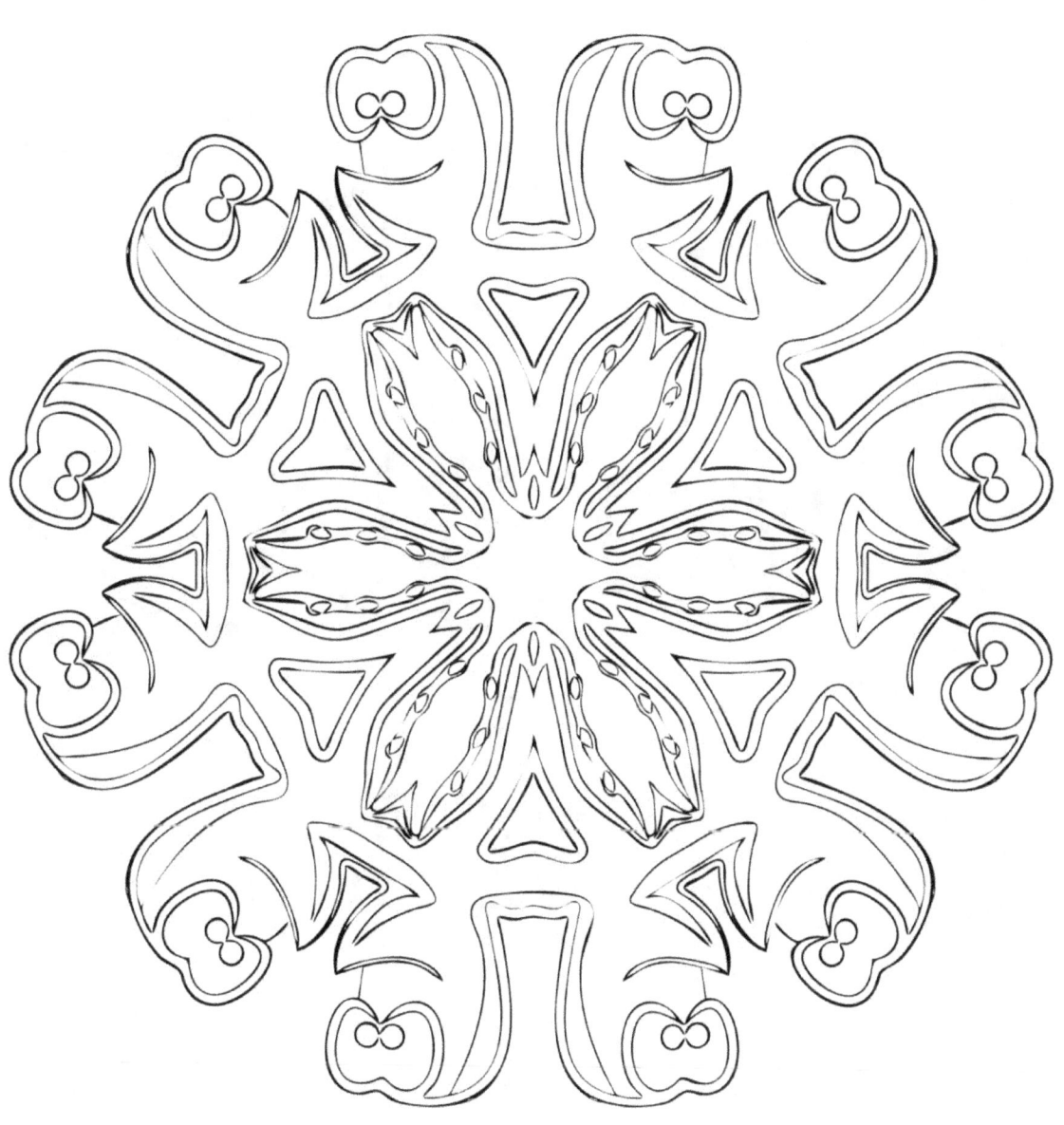

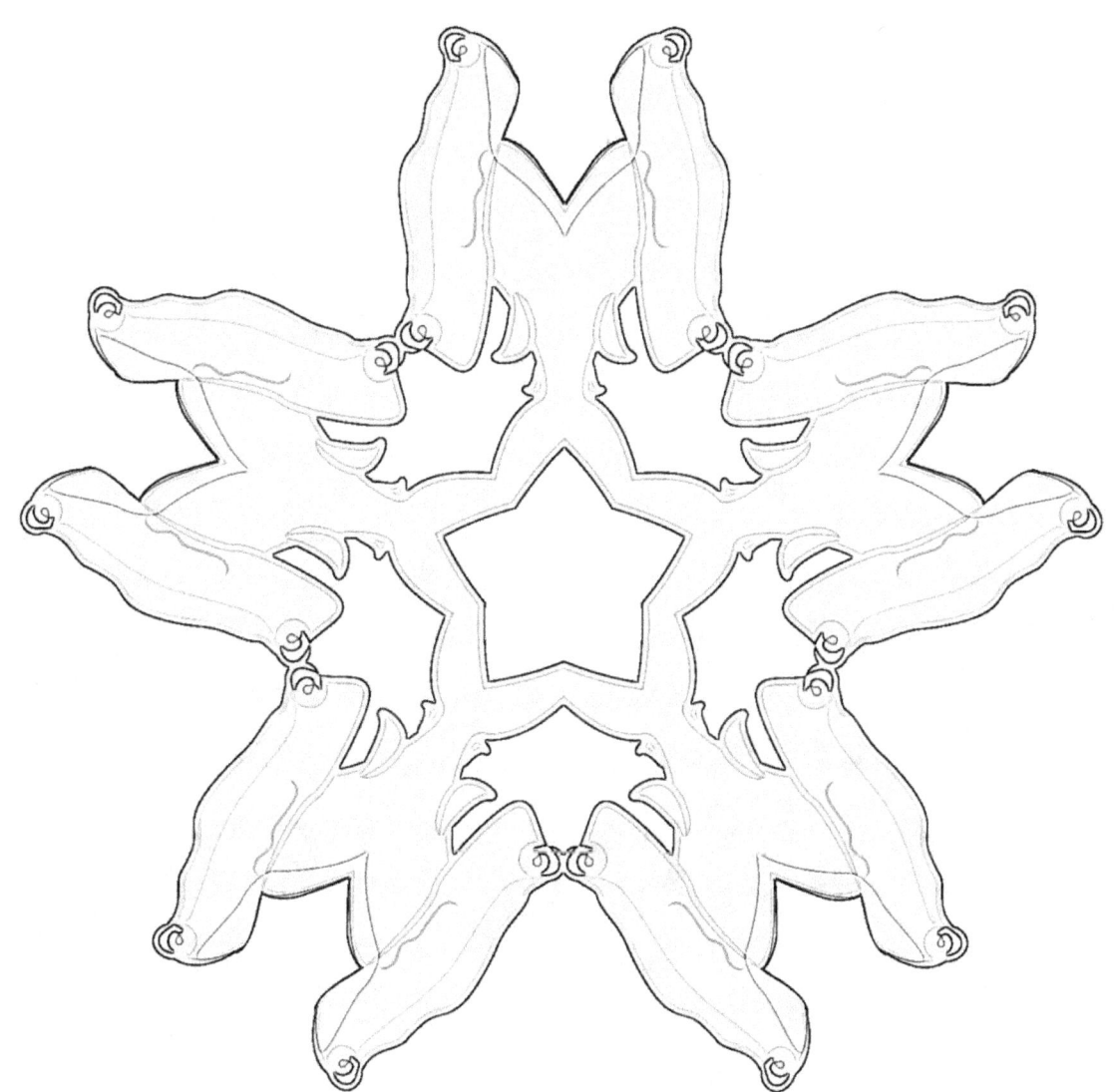

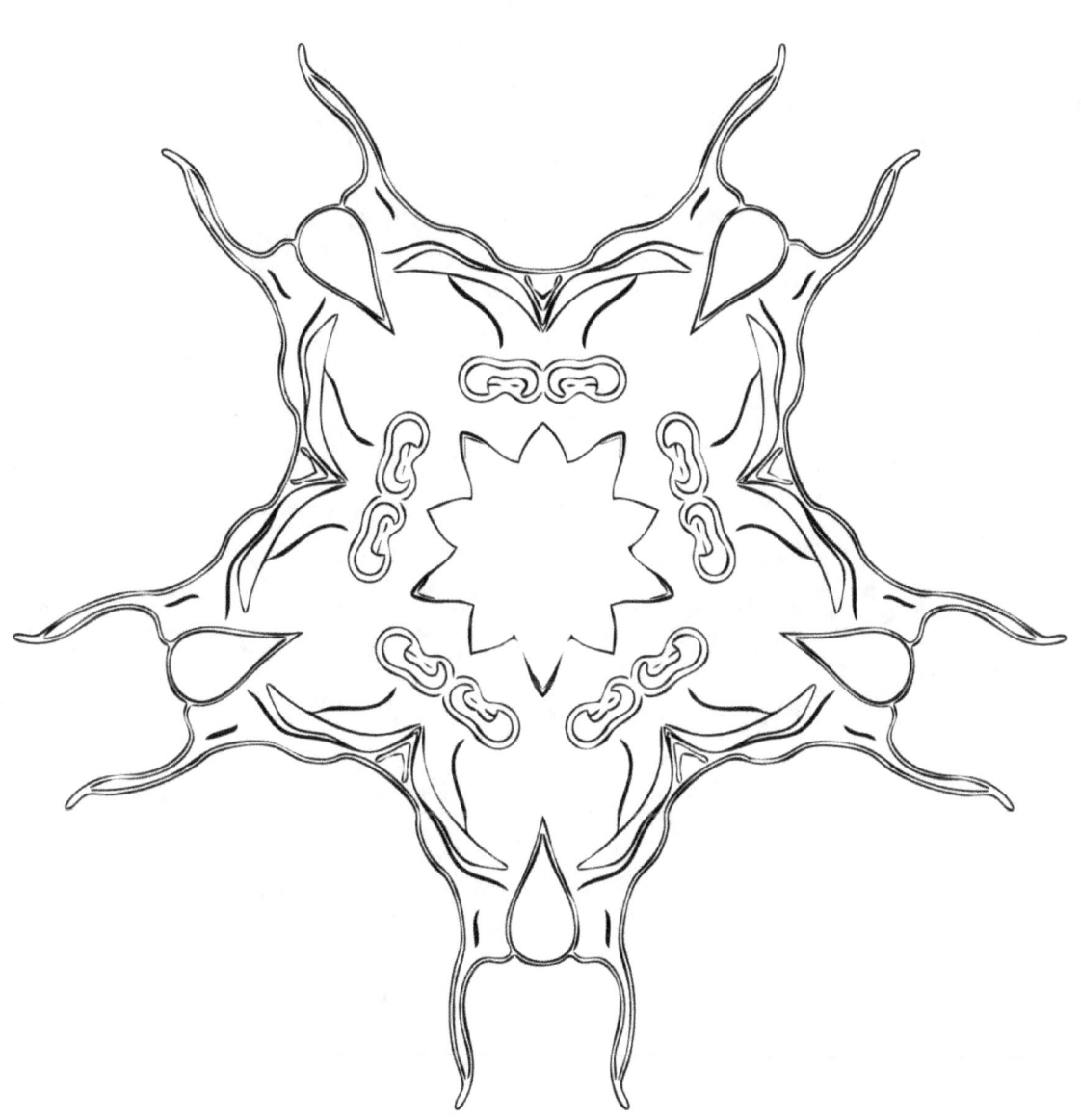

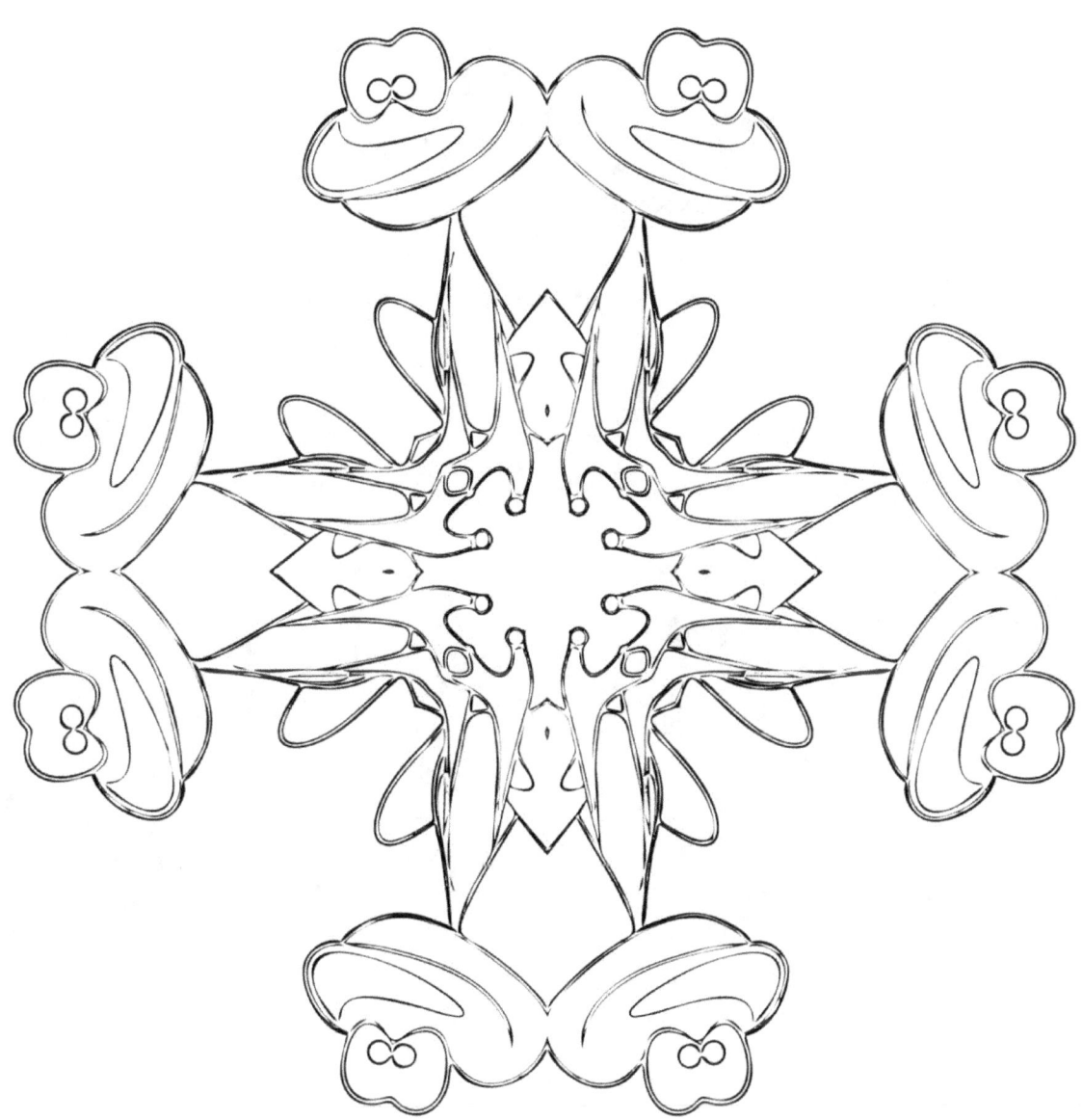

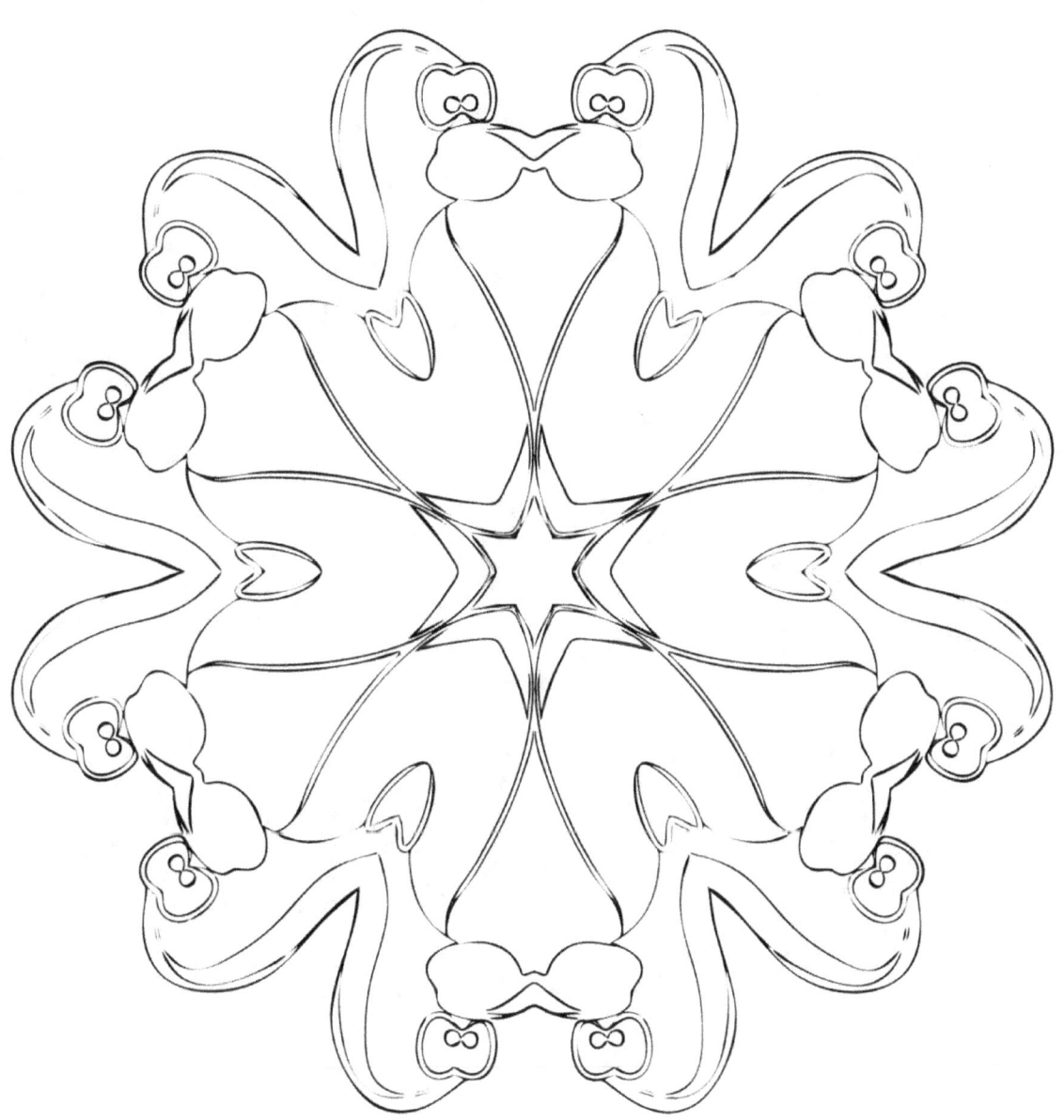

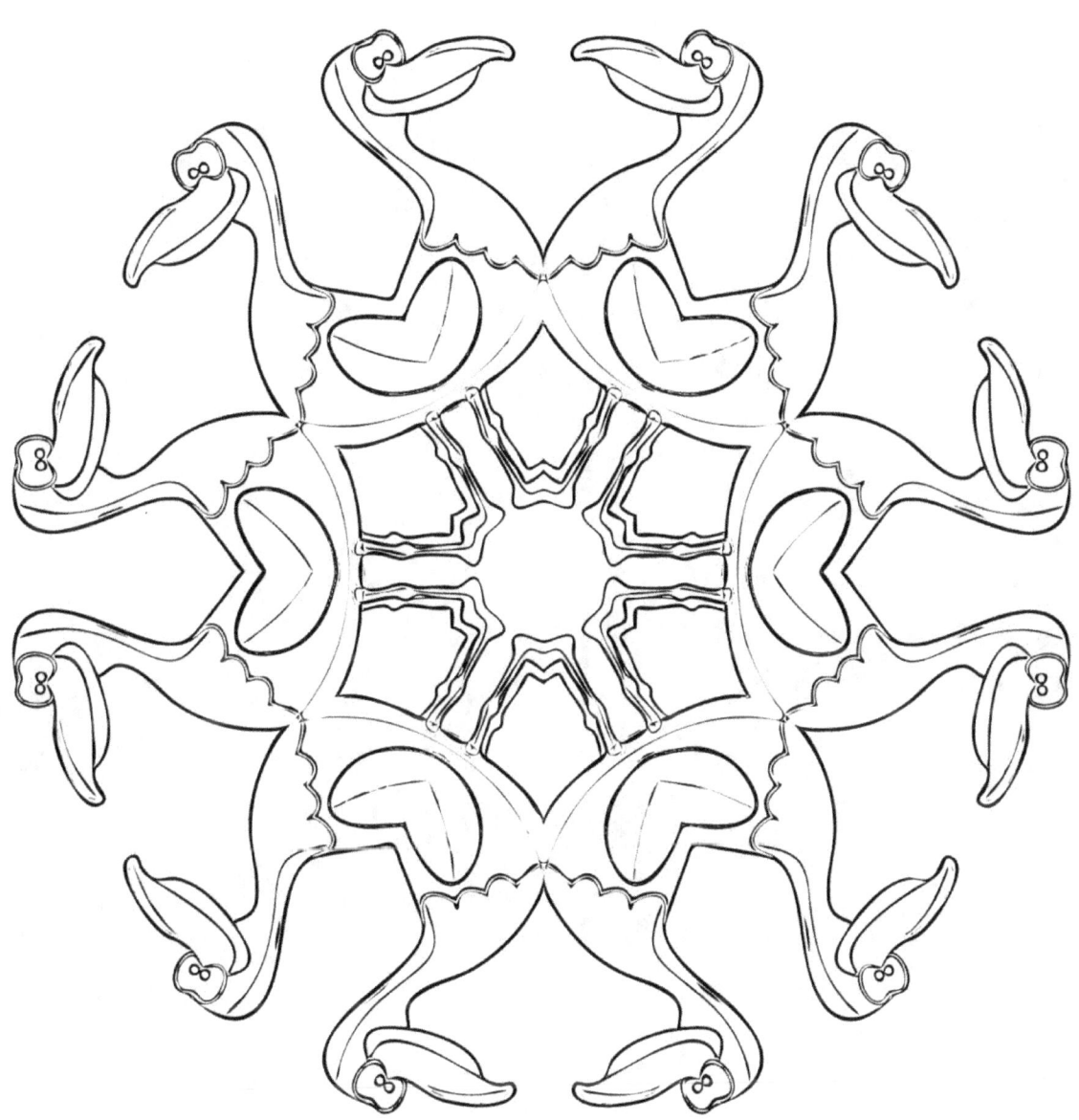

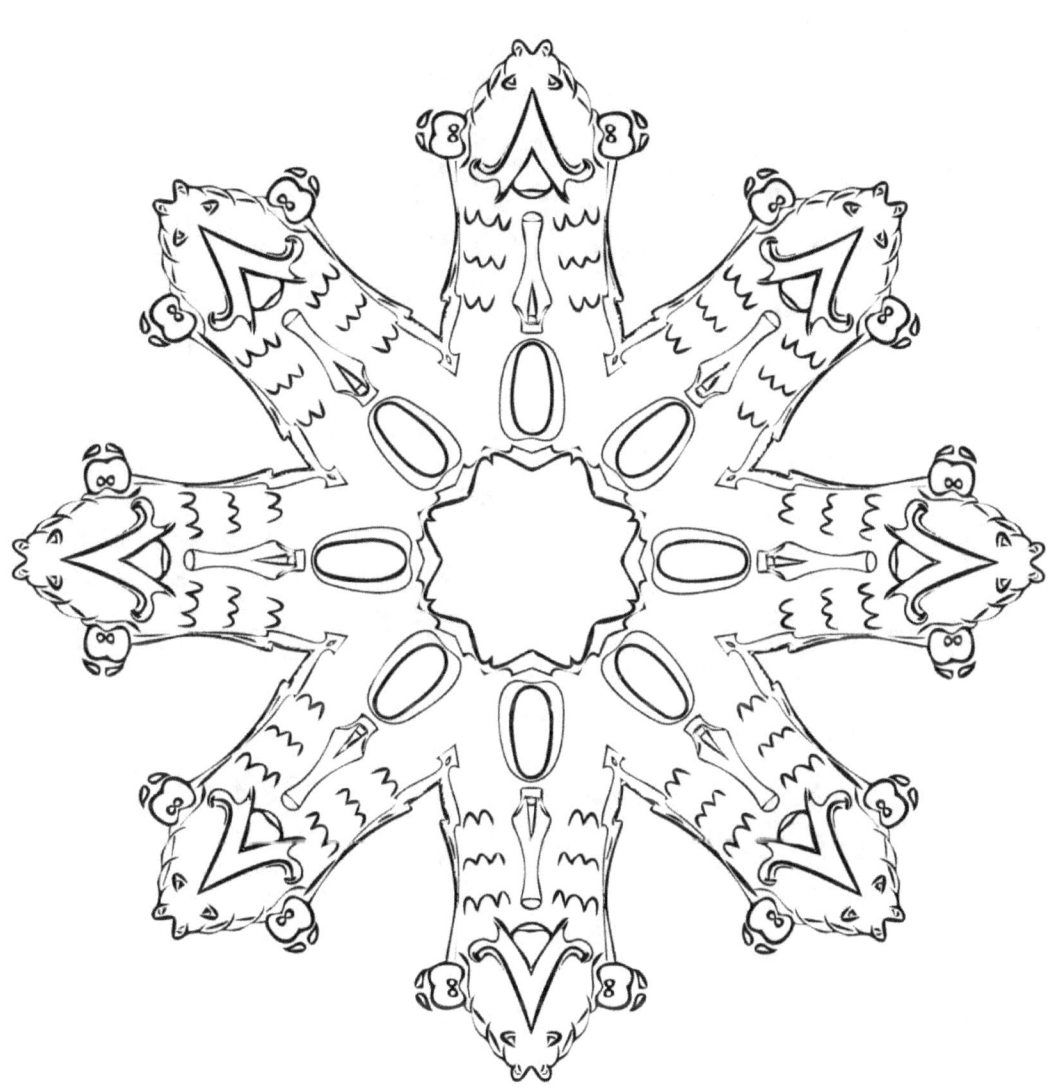

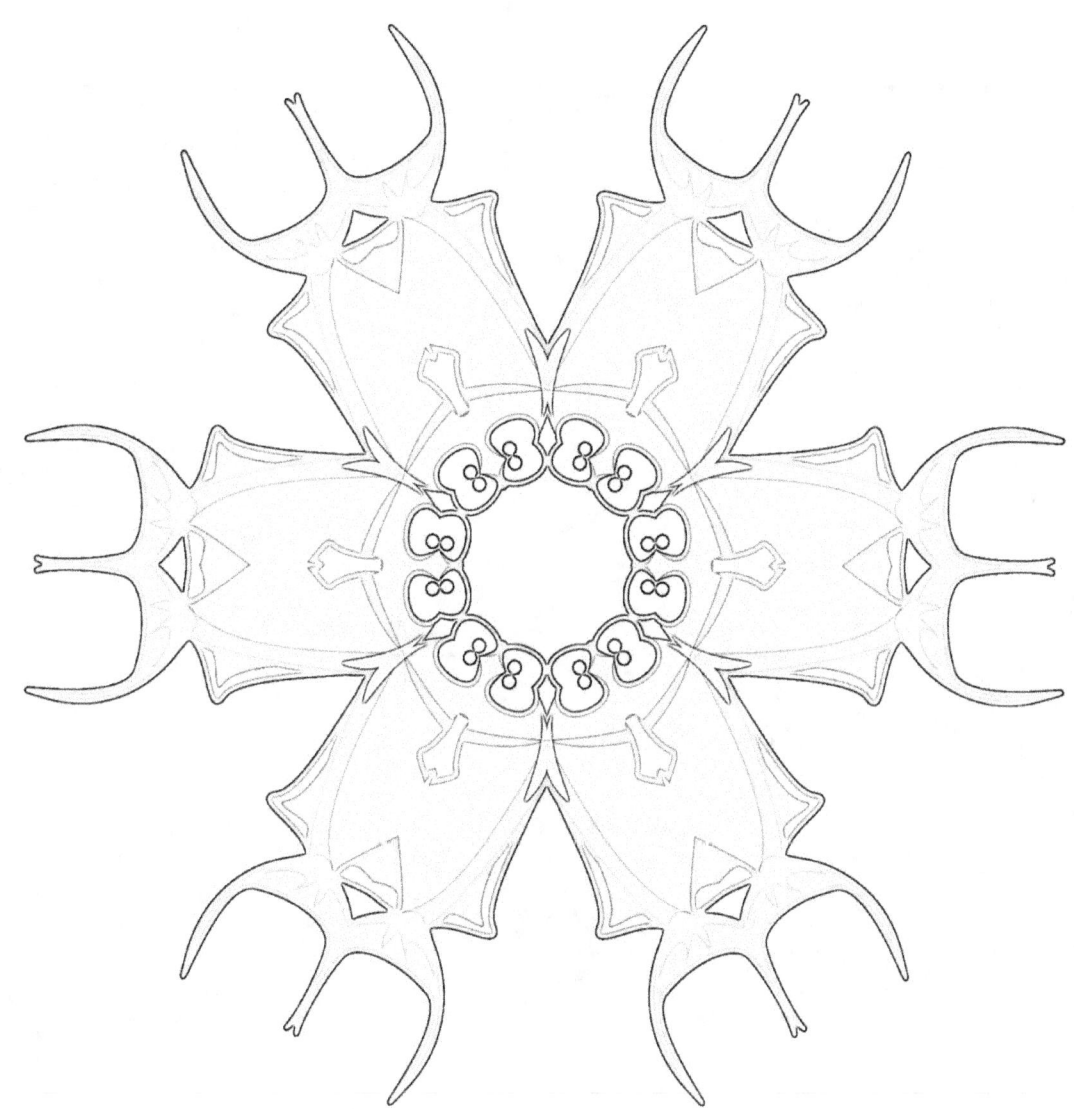

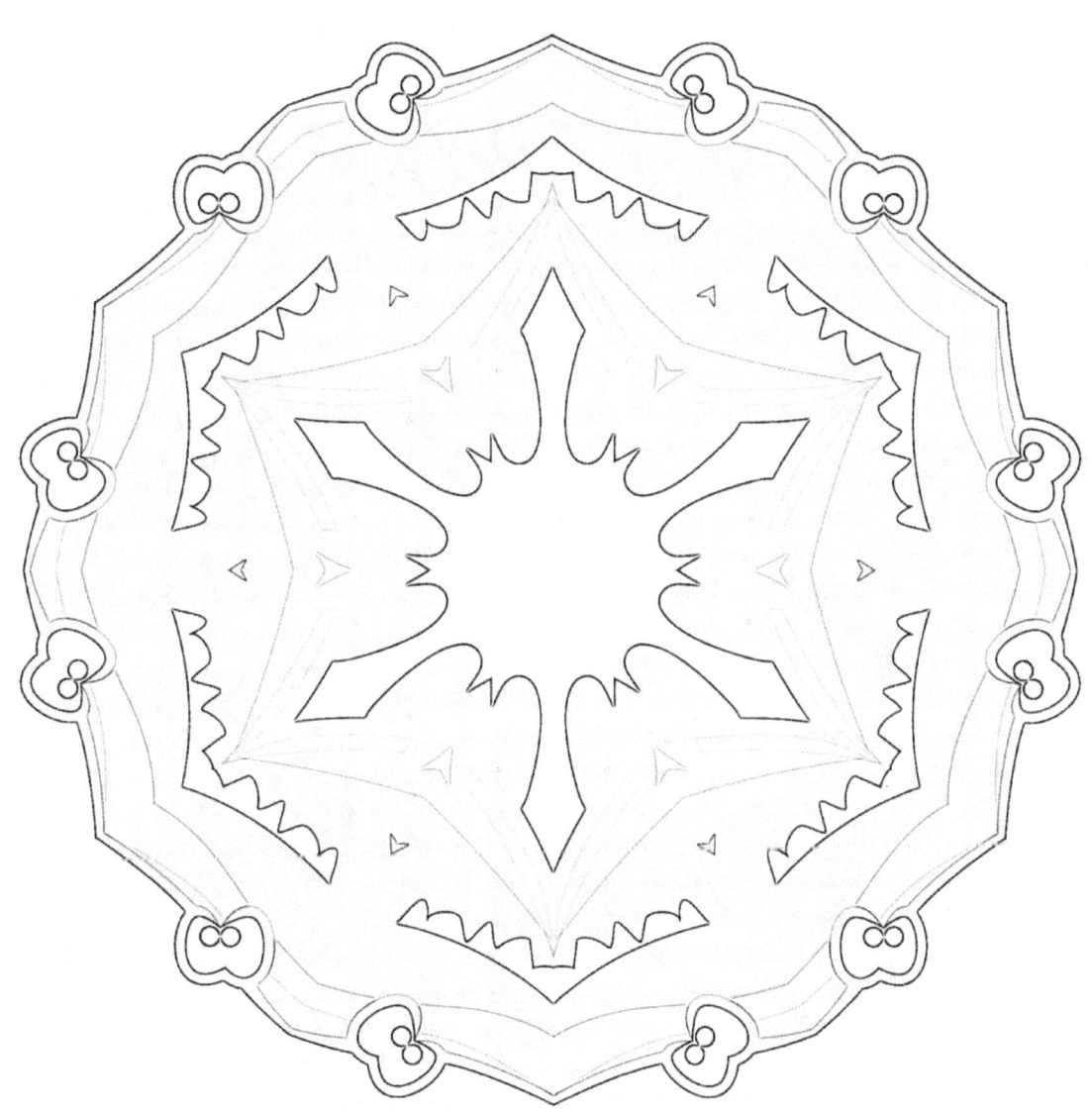

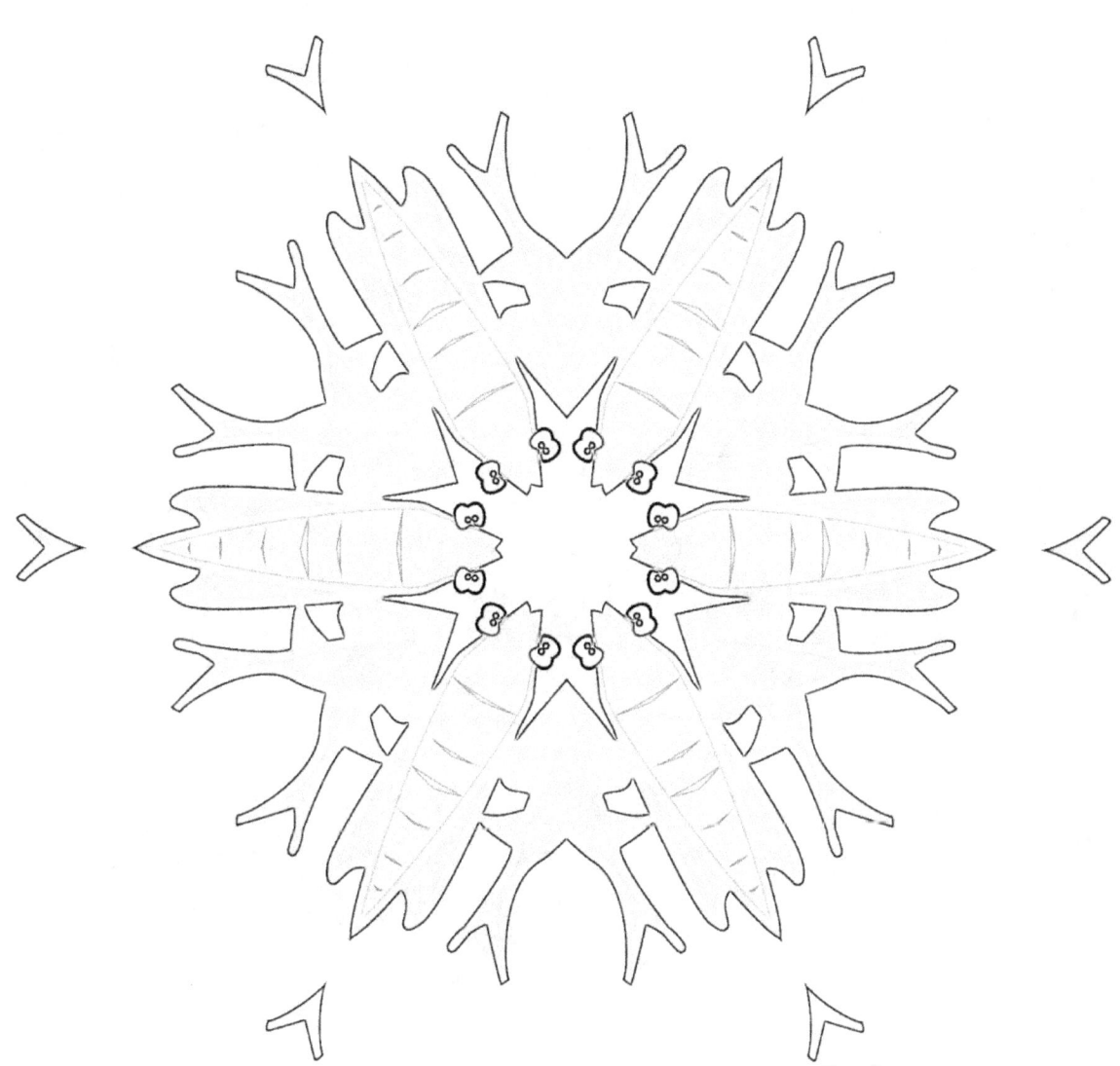

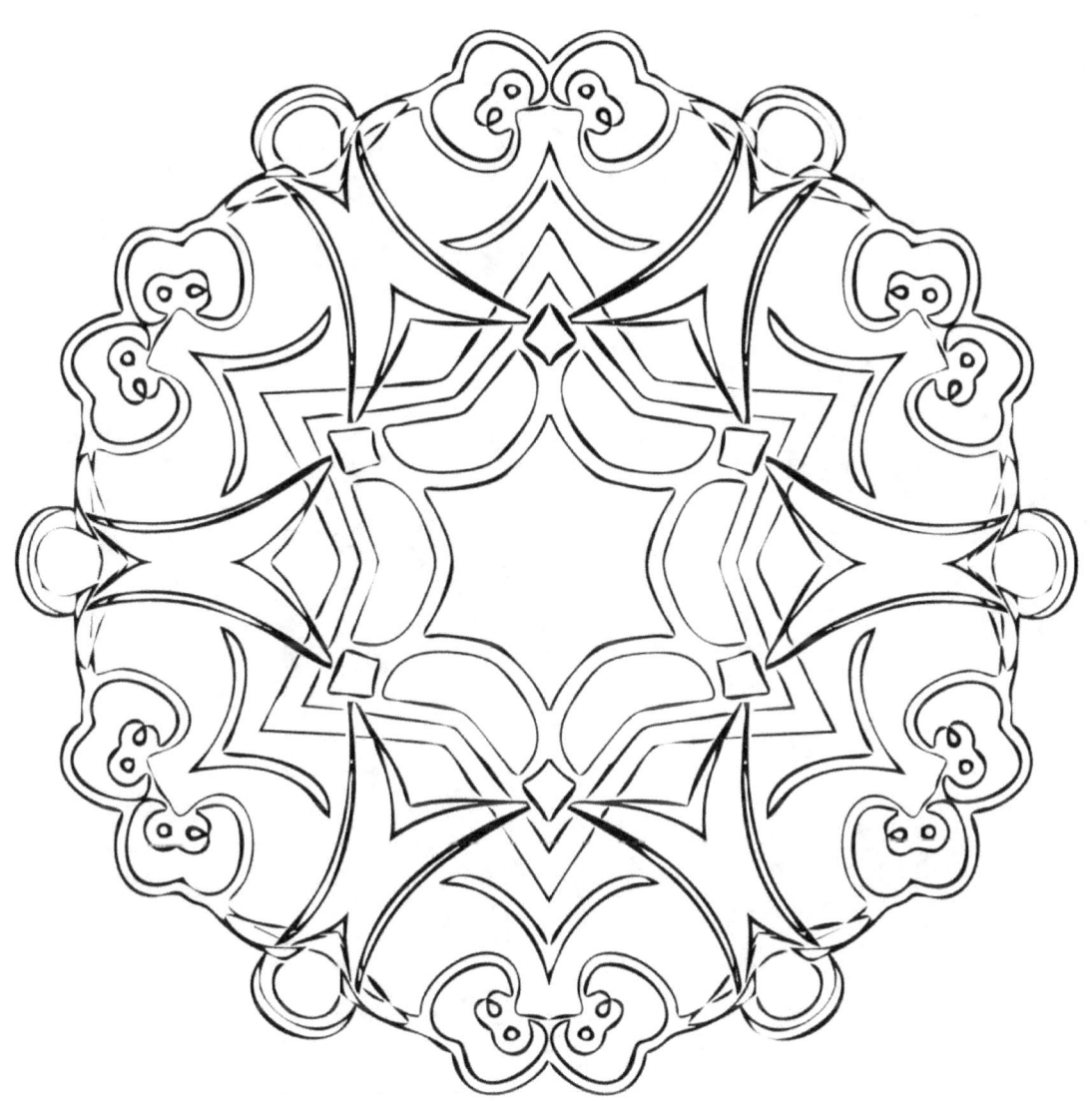

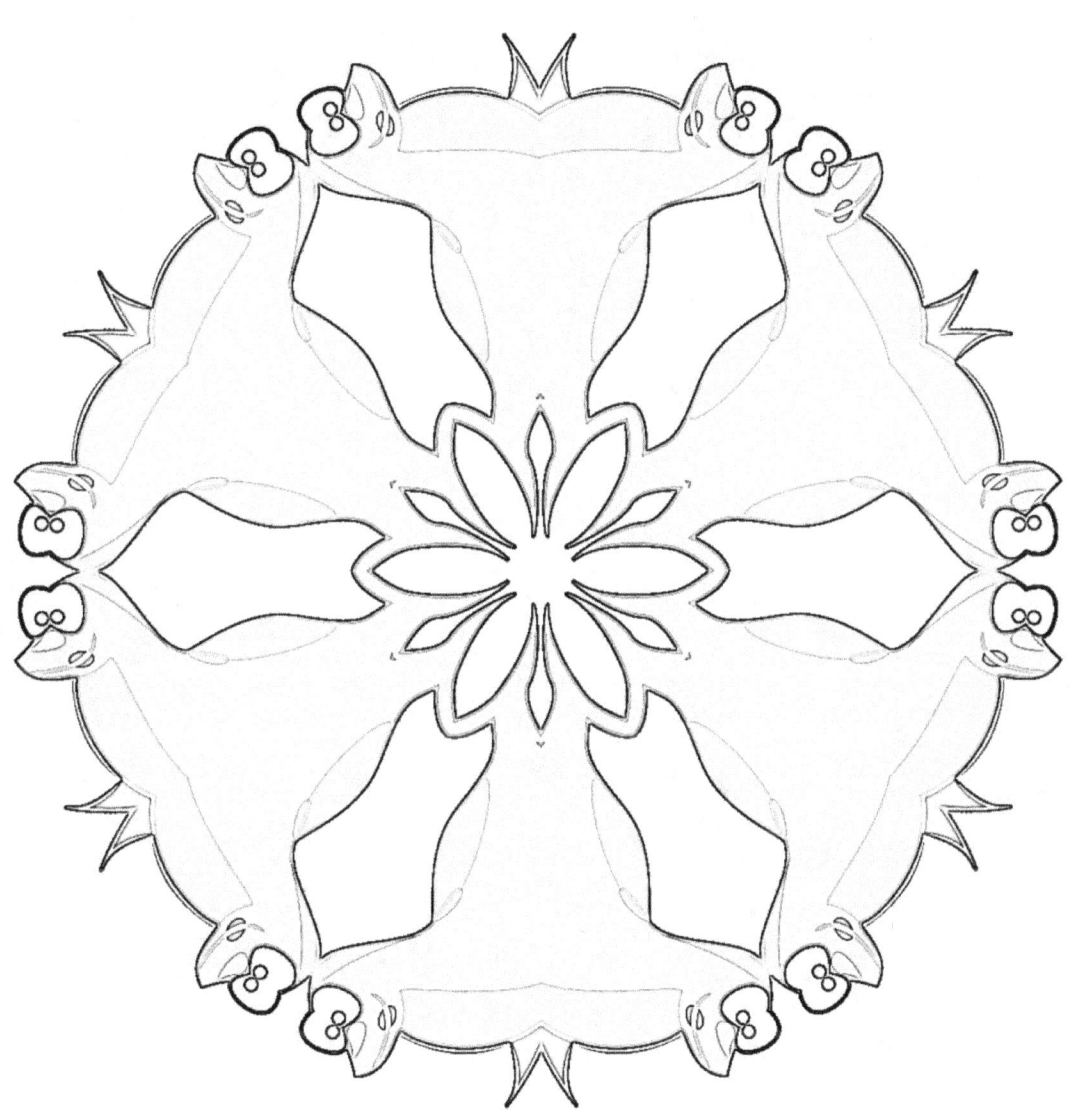

www.ingramcontent.com/pod-product-compliance
Lightning Source LLC
Chambersburg PA
CBHW080806180526
45168CB00006B/2337